NEOPATRIARCHY

NEOPATRIARCHY

A Theory of Distorted Change
in Arab Society

Hisham Sharabi

New York   Oxford
OXFORD UNIVERSITY PRESS
1988

Oxford University Press

Oxford   New York   Toronto
Delhi   Bombay   Calcutta   Madras   Karachi
Petaling Jaya   Singapore   Hong Kong   Tokyo
Nairobi   Dar es Salaam   Cape Town
Melbourne   Auckland

and associated companies in
Berlin   Ibadan

Published by Oxford University Press, Inc.,
200 Madison Avenue, New York, New York 10016

Oxford is a registered trademark of Oxford University Press

Library of Congress Cataloging-in-Publication Data

Sharabi, Hisham, 1927–
Neopatriarchy : a theory of distorted change in Arab society / by
Hisham Sharabi
p.   cm.
Includes index.
ISBN 0-19-505141-6
1. Arab countries—Social conditions.   2. Social structures—Arab
countries.   3. Patriarchy—Arab countries.   4. Sex role—Arab
countries.   5. Social change.   I. Title.
HN766.A8S434 1988
306'.0917'4927—dc 19
87-34876
CIP

2 4 6 8 9 7 5 3 1

Printed in the United States of America
on acid-free paper

For Nadia and Leyla

Preface

Armed young men at a barricade on a main highway; they stop cars and check identity cards. From a car they pull two men, one a youth in his early twenties, the other middle-aged, both belonging to the "wrong" religious sect. The two are pushed to the side of the road. On their knees, crying and begging for mercy, they are shot in cold blood.

This is not a fictional scene; it is almost a normal occurrence in a civil war still taking place in one of the most modern of the Arab countries, the so-called Switzerland of the Middle East. In its own violent way this scene, besides graphically illustrating the disintegration of Lebanon, gives the clue to the unraveling of the larger Arab society I call neopatriarchal society. There are of course other scenes and other aspects equally symptomatic of the processes of social, political, and moral decay: political despotism, corruption, the waste of oil wealth, the inter-Arab wars, the Iran-Iraq war, Israel's humiliating hegemony, Egypt's submissiveness.

The frustrations and humiliations, the rage and despair engendered by this state of affairs have led, since 1948, but particularly since 1967, to the paralyzing trauma engulfing the Arab world. Self-sacrifice (suicide car bombers), mindless violence, escape abroad, or internal exile have now become a way out for many. The depths of self-hatred and cynicism equal only the ethnocentric fantasies and wild dreams of past glory.

What is the cause of this abject helplessness, this hopeless disunity, this global collapse? Is it just Zionism, colonialism, imperialism? Or is it something else, something at the heart of the society, some invisible disease eating at the center?

Arab commentators have become experts at dissecting the terminal condition. But what is needed is more than verbal outbursts venting bitterness and frustration: an analytical framework providing the ground for a systematic interpretation. The need for a theoretical approach has increased as the crisis has become more entrenched and more intractable. As data have piled up, the overall picture has become increasingly opaque and incoherent. We have now reached the point where we can no longer make out the forest for the trees. My attempt here is to provide a framework in which the diverse facts, events, and aspects of social and political phenomena can be organized and made sense of.

Methodologically, this attempt will involve taking an approach and using concepts that may go against assumptions and positions that have been largely taken for granted, as well as taking intellectual risks—engaging in interdisciplinary analyses conducted on different levels, often from opposing ideological positions. And perhaps what makes for the greatest risk is the implicit ambition to influence reality—the conviction that critical discourse can itself be an instrument of change. This critique aspires to contribute to possible forms of praxis, forms necessitated not by mere scholarly interest but by concrete exigencies—a situation in which the critical moment calls on critical theory to play some socially meaningful role.

Some readers will probably object to a critique of Arab society grounded in concepts and models not directly based on Arab or Muslim thought but derived from different theories and different social-historical experiences; such an approach, it may be said, would lead to eclecticism or to an exogenous interpretation. I have decided to take this risk. As we proceed, I shall elucidate my strategy of interpretation—and, I hope,

[handwritten margin note: Why not use local theory? D/c social theories are part of the mindset he wants to explain.]

also justify it. But I should like now to make clear that this attempt is premised on the necessity of transcending neopatriarchal consciousness and of providing independent bases for its critique. My assumption is that only by going beyond and outside the prevailing neopatriarchal paradigm can we adequately grasp and criticize the reality and inner structures of this society. The neopatriarchal discourse, whether in its religious or secular mode—including the nationalist and leftist variants—is necessarily delimited by the horizon of the dominant neopatriarchal paradigm. My purpose is precisely to breach this horizon, and to bring alternative concepts and categories, and other kinds of analysis and criticism, to bear on both neopatriarchal reality and its paradigmatic structures.

It remains to be said that my attempt starts from a position lying within social reality itself, not from an Archimedean position located outside it. I have no apologies to make regarding "objectivity." I believe that there is an extra-academic function to scholarship which can be the means for fresh understanding and a powerful vehicle for cultural criticism. My aim is not just to catalogue the different attributes of neopatriarchal society/culture, but to contribute to its dismantling, by suggesting different perspectives of analysis and a different vocabulary which other Arab critics may find useful in deconstructing neopatriarchy as a total cultural phenomenon.

The following considerations will give an idea of how I will go about developing my exposition. I will try, to begin with, to avoid the culture-personality approach; when I emphasize psychological categories (for example, in Chapter 4), I will try not to lose sight of the sociohistorical ground of all such categories. "Culture," "mind," "personality," "national character," viewed as stable and permanent traits or characteristics by Orientalists and modernization theorists, are excluded from this perspective, which tends more to Marxian and Hegelian conceptions of society and history. However, my perspective highlights culture and stresses superstructural elements more than economy, because my primary concern is the centered circle of neopatriarchy as a social and discursive paradigm. In this view, therefore, Max Weber's ideas are no longer opposed to those of Marx but complement them and are anticipated by them. Weber provides a valuable sociological perspective, which parallels that supplied by Freudian psychoanalysis, on the social and cultural phenomena with which Marx is concerned from a historical materialist position (see, for example, Chapters 2 and 3). My intention is not to reconcile the differences implicit in these approaches, but to try to bring them together in a coherent framework to provide a comprehensive view of the basic structures and relations of the social whole.

I should perhaps add that the epistemological debate generated by structuralist and post-structuralist writings has little direct impact on my approach. This is not to say that I do not see its relevance to the critique I am attempting in these pages; on the contrary, I will incorporate some of post-structuralism's basic themes in my analysis of radical criticism and of the kinds of social action that might be possible under neopatriarchy, but without abandoning my "conventional" position, which takes history as real and the "out there" as intelligible. My feeling is that while the intellectual world of late capitalism perhaps can accommodate without much damage the aestheticism and skepticism of a Foucault or a Derrida, the intellectuals of the post-colonial periphery, including the Arab world, can ill afford the risk of philosophical and anti-theoretic skeptimism; and even were they to take this risk, it would—probably—only lead them to political paralysis.

The word modernity, misused and overused by both Western social science and media, has lost its proper signification. As I use it here it denotes a *mode of being,* not a model to aspire to or an example to imitate. For a society not to be modern in the contemporary world exacts a crippling price. It affects not merely its "culture" or "style of life" but the very essence of its mode of existence. Modernity, in one of its most vital aspects, should help both the individual and society realize their greatest potential. My hope is that Arab society will still become modern, will still be able to overcome disabling neopatriarchy and build an independent, progressive, and humane Arab world. This cultural critique is a contribution to that effort.

Washington, D.C.   H. S.
September 1987

Acknowledgments

Some of the ideas and approaches in this study were developed in three courses I have given over the past few years at Georgetown: "Readings in European Intellectual History (Nineteenth and Twentieth Centuries)," "Marx and Freud on History and Society," and "Ideology and Social Change in the Arab World." To a number of my students in those courses I owe very special thanks.

My endeavor to think through the new Arab criticism and its potential for modernity was greatly enriched by discussions in Kuwait, Amman, Cairo, Tunis, and Rabat in 1984, 1985, and 1986 with several Arab writers and intellectuals, many of whose names are mentioned in Chapter 8. To them I extend warm thanks for their hospitality, generosity, and trust.

My special thanks also go to Samih Farsoun and Michael Simpson for reading the manuscript in its entirety and making valuable comments and suggestions; to Connie Holden for generous administrative support; and to Marsha Robinson and Julie Ruterbories for painstaking typing of handwritten drafts.

I would like to express my gratitude to Martha Ramsey for copyediting the manuscript with relentless attention to detail and rare sensitivity to style and content.

This book has been translated into Arabic by Hanna Damian and recast by Ali Ahmad Sa'id (the poet Adonis); to both of them I owe deep gratitude for making this critique available to the audience for which it is primarily intended.

Contents

NEOPATRIARCHY

"Pessimism of the intellect . . .
Optimism of the will . . ."

Romain Rolland as quoted by
Antonio Gramsci

1

Neopatriarchy:
Concept and Reality

Neopatriarchy

As with all interpretive key-concepts, the category of neopatriarchy runs the risk of reductionism: whether or not I shall succeed in escaping this risk, partially or fully, will soon become evident. It would be helpful at the outset to make clear what I intend by the term neopatriarchy.

As I shall use the term in this essay, I have in mind a concept with several aspects and several uses, each determined by its context: an analytical category, an ideal type or model, an interpretive principle, a formal theory. The concept refers equally to macrostructures (society, the state, the economy) and to microstructures (the family or the individual personality).

As it occurs in history, the phenomenon of neopatriarchy derives its meaning from the two terms or realities which make up its concrete structure, *modernity* and *patriarchy*—the specific relationship of which we shall discuss in Chapter 2. Suffice it to note here that the latter term refers to a universal form of traditional society, which assumes a different character in each society, while the former points to a unique historical development which occurred in its original form in Western Europe—the first historical break with traditionality. This unique transformation, in going beyond patriarchy, constituted it and, by the same movement, established the distinction, vital for our discussion, between traditional patriarchy and modernized patriarchy. The latter must be viewed as the product of a hegemonic modern Europe; but "modernization" as the product of patriarchal and dependent conditions can only be dependent "modernization": dependency relations inevitably lead not to modernity but to "modernized" patriarchy, *neopatriarchy*. Modernization, in this context, is the metonomy of inverted modernity.

Thus distinctions made between traditional and progressive, or conservative and radical, in regard to contemporary Arab society ought to be severely qualified. A basic assumption of this study is that over the last one hundred years the patriarchal structures of Arab society, far from being displaced or truly modernized, have only been strengthened and maintained in deformed, "modernized" forms. That is to say, the Arab Awakening or renaissance (*nahda*) of the nineteenth century not only failed to break down the inner relations and forms of patriarchalism but, by initiating what it called the modern awakening, also provided the ground for producing a new, hybrid sort of society/culture—the neopatriarchal society/culture we see before us today. Material modernization, the first (surface) manifestation of social change, only served to remodel and reorganize patriarchal structures and relations and to reinforce them by giving them "modern" forms and appearances.

Neopatriarchy, from the standpoints of both modernity and traditionality, is neither *modern* nor *traditional*—for example, it lacks as a social formation both the communal attributes of *Gemeinschaft* and the modern features of *Gesellschaft*. It is an *entropic* social formation characterized by its transitory nature and by specific kinds of underdevelopment and non-modernity—visible in its economy and class structure as well as its political, social, and cultural organization. Moreover, it is a highly unstable formation, riven by inner contradictions and conflicts—torn, as a contemporary Lebanese writer put it, by "longing, regret, and mourning."[1]

It is impossible to grasp properly the concept of neopatriarchy without recognizing its two implicit and prior terms, patriarchy and dependency.[2] This recognition enables us to understand neopatriarchy as a totality—in its social, economic, political, and cultural aspects—and to see it as a concrete historical formation shaped simultaneously by internal and external forces. From this standpoint the methodological (and ideological) problem posed by the opposition of "internalist" versus "externalist" points of view is overcome and replaced by a unified perspective based on the conjunction of the two.

A basic question emerges when we face the problem of modernization in the context of the Western-dominated world market: Is modernization possible without capitalist development? The classical theory of social change, in both its Marxian and Weberian forms, presents capitalism as a necessary phase of the transformation of society; but while Marx linked capitalism to modernization in the context of "revolution," Weber approached it in terms of "rationalization." As far as the non-European world is concerned, both believed that capitalism—as a "revolutionizing" or "rationalizing" force—was exportable, and that the replacement of traditional, nonrational structures by modern ones would inevitably follow upon the introduction of commodity exchange and the capitalist mode of production. Neither foresaw the development of a *dependent* capitalism, the only form of capitalism—as seen in retrospect—historically possible in the wake of European capitalism and in a Western-dominated world market.

In the Arab world, capitalism, introduced into Egypt and the Fertile Crescent in the nineteenth and early twentieth centuries, far from providing the conditions for the development of autonomous capitalism, produced the political and economic conditions of distorted, dependent capitalism. Under this kind of "peripheral" capitalism it was impossible for a full-fledged bourgeoisie and genuine working class to develop; a hybrid social class, distinct from both the underdeveloped bourgeoisie and proletariat, developed into a dominant class

by the mid-twentieth century. The consciousness of this class,
like its social structure, reflected neither the conditions of the
bourgeoisie nor those of the urban workers, but a unique
amalgam with nonproletarian emphasis. I call this hybrid class
simply the neopatriarchal petty bourgeoisie and its consciousness neopatriarchal: just as the neopatriarchal social formation is characterized by the peculiar mode of production of
dependent capitalism, so the petty bourgeoisie may be defined
as the hybrid, dominant class characteristic of neopatriarchal
society.

The *Nahda* and Neopatriarchal Society

If the term *nahda* were to be stretched to cover the period
from the mid or late nineteenth century—the point at which
the West's impact became a central factor in Arab sociopolitical life—to the present, it would coincide with neopatriarchal
society. This temporal span may be divided into three main
periods: the Ottoman period, which comes to an end with the
First World War; the period of European political domination, which falls between the two World Wars (earlier in
North Africa and Egypt); and the postindependence period,
from the Second World War to the present.

Recall that the first period (the Ottoman), with its anteced-
ents, marks the dividing line between two historical epochs:
the "age of decline," which begins with the disintegration of
the Abbassid empire in the thirteenth century, and the "modern age." Yet this description fails to account for the fact that
except for ushering in certain material forms of modernization, the Awakening in effect did not constitute a general cultural break in the sense the European renaissance did; for on
the one hand, it did not achieve a genuine transcendence of
inherited structures of thought and social (including economic
and political) organization, and on the other, it failed to grasp
the true nature of modernity. and to?

Neopatriarchal society as a dependent, nonmodern socioeconomic structure represents the quintessentially underdeveloped society. Its most pervasive characteristic is a kind of generalized, persistent, and seemingly insurmountable impotence: it is incapable of performing as an integrated social or political system, as an economy, or as a military structure. Possessing all the external trappings of modernity, this society nevertheless lacks the inner force, organization, and consciousness which characterize truly modern formations. Indeed, modernization in this context is for the most part only a mechanism promoting underdevelopment and social entropy, which in turn produce and reproduce the hybrid, traditional, and semi-rational structures and consciousness typical of neopatriarchal society.

A central psychosocial feature of this type of society, whether it is conservative or progressive, is the dominance of the Father (patriarch), the center around which the national as well as the natural family are organized. Thus between ruler and ruled, between father and child, there exist only vertical relations: in both settings the paternal will is the absolute will, mediated in both the society and the family by a forced consensus based on ritual and coercion. Significantly, the most advanced and functional aspect of the neopatriarchal state (in both conservative and "progressive" regimes) is its internal security apparatus, the *mukhabarat*. A two-state system prevails in all neopatriarchal regimes, a military-bureaucratic structure alongside a secret police structure, and the latter dominates everyday life, serving as the ultimate regulator of civil and political existence. Thus in social practice ordinary citizens not only are arbitrarily deprived of some of their basic rights but are the virtual prisoners of the state, the objects of its capricious and ever-present violence, much as citizens once were under the classical or Ottoman sultanate. As we shall see, the neopatriarchal state, regardless of its legal and political forms and structures, is in many ways no more than a modernized version of the traditional patriarchal sultanate.

As for the *civic* space where one may seek to distance one-

self and find shelter from naked power—the primary institutions of family, clan, or religious sect—these too, one always
discovers, display similar forms of authority and violence.
Thus whatever the outward ("modern") forms—material, legal, aesthetic—of the contemporary neopatriarchal family and
society, their internal structures remain rooted in the patriarchal values and social relations of kinship, clan, and religious and ethnic groups. In a peculiar duality, the modern and
the patriarchal coexist in contradictory union.

Neopatriarchy's schizophrenic duality manifests itself most
clearly in the petty bourgeoisie, the social class most representative of neopatriarchal society and culture. In this class can
be found the most contradictory values and tendencies co-
existing without conscious resolution or synthesis, producing
the kind of disjointed and contradictory structures and practices that are most typical of this society. The following portrayal by the Egyptian novelist Nagib Mahfouz of one of his
petty bourgeois characters provides a glimpse of this contradictory world.

> He leads a contemporary [i.e., "modern"] life. He obeys civil and
> penal laws of Western origin and is involved in a complex tangle of
> social and economic transactions and is never certain to what extent
> these agree with or contradict his Islamic creed. Life carries him
> along in its current and he forgets his misgivings for a time until
> one Friday he hears the imam or reads the religious page in one
> of the papers, and the old misgivings come back with a certain fear.
> He realizes that in this new society he has been afflicted with a split
> personality: half of him believes, prays, fasts and makes the pil-
> grimage. The other half renders his values void in banks and courts
> and in the streets, even in the cinemas and theaters, perhaps even
> at home among his family before the television set.[3]

The Rise of the Neopatriarchal Petty Bourgeoisie

The petty bourgeoisie's rise to dominance resulted from two
main developments: the population explosion of the 1940s
and 1950s, which accelerated the movement to the cities and
augmented the ranks of the urban petty bourgeoisie; and the

seizure of power by petty bourgeois army officers and political party leaders during the post-World War II era in the four core countries of the Arab world: Egypt, Syria, Iraq, and Algeria. It soon became clear that the new class, embodied in its leadership, was an ineffective social force, lacking internal unity and coherence and utterly incapable of carrying out the tasks either of the bourgeoisie (i.e., capitalist economic development) or the proletariat (i.e., revolutionary social transformation). Petty bourgeois rule now exposed both these classes, whose development had been stunted by dependency and imperialism, to further enfeeblement. The bourgeoisie has been politically disenfranchised and uprooted, and the petty bourgeoisie has patronized and controlled the urban proletariat and absorbed it into its culture.

Under the hegemony of the petty bourgeoisie not only did the revolution and Arab unity suffer defeat, but political life in the Arab world disintegrated into domestic authoritarianism and rivalry between antagonistic regimes. The movement of social change and development faltered, leading by the 1970s to a kind of state-capitalist consumer society in the "progressive" states and a distorted free-market capitalism in the conservative ones.[4] Petty bourgeois rule in the former (and its cultural dominance in the latter) contributed to the spread of a peculiar kind of anomie, giving rise to a clear class split between the new petty bourgeois power elite in the "progressive" regimes (in the conservative regimes, the new rich) and the underprivileged and increasingly alienated petty bourgeois-proletarian masses. This split brought with it a significant ideological reorientation exemplified by the spread of a militant and politicized Islamic fundamentalism among the Arab masses.

Islamic Fundamentalism and Secular Modernism

In its basic dimension modernity is a transitional process involving a movement from one mode of knowledge or paradig-

matic structure to another radically different, a break with
traditional (mythical) ways of understanding reality in favor
of new (scientific) modes of thought. In Arab society this process was experienced in terms of three basic problematics: the
problematic of *identity*, the problematic of *history*, and the
problematic of European civilization or the *West*. The Arab
Awakening, in its main preoccupations, may be seen as a cultural and social struggle between the two fundamental standpoints of secularism and Islam. The first took the West as its
implicit or explicit model, and the second adhered to Islam as
its source of legitimacy and inspiration. Secularism (expressed
in liberalism, nationalism, and socialism) and fundamentalism
(articulated in reformist, conservative, and militant Islam)
provided the Awakening's two basic "regimes of truth," which
went on to dominate the subsequent phases of neopatriarchal
society. In retrospect, we can see that neither secularism nor
Islamism succeeded in developing a genuinely independent
critical and analytical discourse in which the problematics of
identity, history and the West could find effective resolution.

   The Islamic trend, in its reformist as well as conservative
and militant forms, viewed history and the West in ideological terms and could see the past only as the embodiment or
repository of the Truth of Islam and its golden age, and the
West as the negation of both. From this position a truly modern reading of the past[5] was clearly impossible, as was the ability to come realistically to terms with the Self and the Other.
In time only a radical fundamentalist view in the face not
only of secularism but also reformist and established Islam,
would be able to claim absolute validity, as it does today, as
the interpreter of self, history and society. The secularist discourse, also based on an ideological stance, but grounded in
nationalism, liberalism, and "science" rather than religion,
regarded the past as a *value*, implying *identity* and *power*
(superiority of the national heritage), the two preconditions
for dealing with the admired/feared Other. So the search for
or affirmation of *identity*, in both its Islamic and secularist

forms, took place in a political-cultural space where *history* and the *West* were intertwined opposites; each side tried to invoke its respective pole to validate itself and provide a foundation for its own vision of identity, in Islam or Arabism.

Fundamentalism and Secular Criticism

In the late 1980s these contending discourses seem to have reached a climax. Islamism is no longer represented by a peripheral group but constitutes a mass grassroots movement, while secularism still consists of an internally diverse, largely avant-garde movement of critical intellectuals, writers, professionals, scholars, and students. Until about mid-century, the intellectual and cultural debate was largely confined to the educated circles of the urban centers. With the most recent social transformation, the participants in the debate, and its very substance, have changed. At this juncture, the stakes involve not just the outcome of a theoretical encounter but the very fate of society.

My contention is that though Islamic fundamentalism may be able to contain the anomic manifestations of neopatriarchal society, it can offer no cure for the structural disorders of that society, of which, at this terminal stage, anomie is the most pervasive symptom. Essentially idealistic, fundamentalism will address only symptoms, and its solutions will necessarily be authoritarian, based on absolutist doctrine and methods. Thus at the same time that fundamentalism may appear as a liberating force, it will inevitably be oppressive: as it violently brings down neopatriarchal society (or ineluctably decomposes it from within) it will inexorably retreat toward authoritarian patriarchy.

In this context, the new movement of secular criticism appears to be the direct political and cultural antithesis of Islamic fundamentalism. The way the two discourses, secular or radical criticism and Islamic fundamentalism, confront each other may be summarized in this formulation:

On one hand an absolutist, traditionalist position, on the other a self-limiting, rationalizing position.

Total hegemony facing free pluralism.

An ethic of ultimate ends confronting an ethic of responsibility.

A monological discourse facing a dialogical discourse.

Secular criticism's fatal weakness lies in that, unlike fundamentalism, it is an avant-garde movement and out of touch with the masses. As such it finds itself at a double disadvantage: it enjoys limited power in the political arena (lacking political organization), and as state censorship erodes, restricts, and deflects its effectiveness, it finds itself also opposed by mass (religious) opinion. Fundamentalism, on the other hand, is able by means of its religious appeal to put the status quo on the defensive as well as mobilize the masses. But perhaps the greatest drawback the secular critics suffer stems from the fundamentalists' refusal to engage in rational and open discussion. The latter's approach is essentially one of *persuasion* (to "see the true path") or *conversion* (to "return to the true faith") rather than debate, reasoning, or argument. Thus secular criticism is reduced to the status of a heretical or subversive discourse, and the radical critics are pushed back to the position of defensive interlocutors who lack legitimacy. It is fair perhaps to conclude that the moment fundamentalism gains power it will tend to rule out the possibility of any sort of dialogue.

While the new radical critics are routinely attacked, muzzled, and suppressed in most Arab regimes, fundamentalist spokespersons are not only allowed to proclaim their doctrines freely and publicly but are often provided with substantial aid by the state institutional machinery and media. Fundamentalism derives much of its strength from the vulnerability of the ruling classes, who invoke the same ideology as fundamentalism to validate their own uncertain legitimacy.

Neopatriarchal society and the political and economic structures at its base are deteriorating today before our very eyes. Fundamentalism, in the form of an antimodernist, utopian patriarchalism, sees itself as the legitimate successor of the disintegrating neopatriarchal status quo. The Iranian example, while not taken as the model of Arab Sunni fundamentalism, affirms the feasibility of bringing down the neopatriarchal political order no matter how materially powerful it might appear.

A question central to this critique now presents itself: Given the state of debility and disintegration of contemporary neopatriarchal society, is fundamentalism's victory inevitable, or do the forces of secularism and modernity have a chance?

Each generation sees itself as standing at the end of historical time and so tragically looks to the future to bring some inescapable denouement. Of course, a fundamentalist victory may bring about a new era in the life of this generation, as it did in Iran and may soon in Pakistan or some other Islamic country. However, as we have learned from recent experience, there can be no inevitability about such happenings. Neopatriarchy, as the negation of both authenticity and modernity, stands a good chance of being dismantled or overwhelmed by the activity of critical modernity as well as militant fundamentalism. And if fundamentalism may reject the partnership of the modern critics, the latter may have something to gain from a fundamentalist success. To the extent that fundamentalism is able to dismantle neopatriarchy's structures, it could contribute to realizing modernity's possibilities. One may also look for what survives of the revolutionary and progressive potential within Arab society, particularly as expressed in the new young generation raised in a global, secularized environment. Thus the modernist impulse, simultaneously cultivated and frustrated over the last three generations, may revive and even take political form. And when one remembers that this impulse may not be as tightly bound to conventional revolutionary means as it was a generation ago, a fundamentalist advance may appear that much less threatening and more manageable.

Of course, the outcome of this struggle will not be determined by internal factors alone; in part it will be influenced by the direction world history will take, the superpowers' attitude toward this vital area of the world, and developments in the Third World.

Now let us start from the beginning and try to answer some of the questions raised thus far. The first question is, what constitutes the phenomenon we call neopatriarchy? The starting point is patriarchy.

2

Patriarchy and Modernity

Basic Assumptions

What is patriarchal society? How does it come into being? How is it transformed? What are its distinctive features—its values, forms of knowledge, social practices, political organization? To answer these and other related questions we must first clarify our basic assumptions, which will enable us to see in what sense we take traditional Arab society to be patriarchal.

To begin with, patriarchy is a term that essentially defines a specific kind of social-political structure, with a specific value system and forms of discourse and practice, based on a distinctive mode of economic organization. Patriarchy is the central social relational feature of the precapitalist social formation which has historically existed in varying forms in Europe and Asia. Our contention is that patriarchy took a specific and distinctive form in the society we characterize as traditional Arab society. So while some of the characteristics we will analyze here may fit other, non-Arab societies, their specificity is derived from the conditions, development, and experiences belonging to the Arab world.

Basically, the same historical uniqueness as pertains to other distinctive cultures—the Indian, Chinese, Japanese, or Western European—bestows historical specificity on Arab patriarchy. For despite historically similar socioeconomic determinants, all these cultures passed through formative experiences that were determined by specific geographical, climatic, and demographic conditions.

So if the character of society and of the men and women who make it up is fashioned in part by the physical environment in which they live, what sort of physical nature gave rise to the peculiar characteristics of Arab patriarchy? Arab culture (Islamic civilization), as Fernand Braudel observes, developed "on the margins of empty spaces, on the edges of deserts, rivers and seas."[1] One glance at the map immediately shows how true this observation is: the dominant feature of this environment is the empty space of the desert, from the Atlantic to the Gulf. The desert dominates the entire Arab world, except for (1) the narrow and discontinuous fringe along the Mediterranean from Alexandretta to Tangiers, (2) the mountain cluster of the Western Maghreb (Atlas), (3) the mountain ranges of geographic Syria, (4) the hinterlands of Oman and Yemen, and (5) the river basins of the Nile and the Euphrates.

The demographic feature is equally striking. Historically, the city dwellers and the bedouin dominated the culture and society (commerce and political power), while the agricultural producers were subordinate to both. This formation is further shaped by the region's geopolitical position astride the two major concentrations of humanity, Europe to the north and west, and Afro-Asia to the south and east. Thus long-distance trade and foreign invasions were *constitutive* for the Arab world's economic and political evolution.

Is there a difference between patriarchal society and "traditional" society? In what sense is it possible to speak of different patriarchal societies? Clearly, patriarchy as a socioeconomic category refers to traditional, premodern society. In this sense, the terms patriarchal society/culture and traditional or premodern society/culture are more or less interchangeable, with both terms being defined in contrast to a *qualitatively* different society/culture—the modern.

In Marx, the "patriarchal condition," the stage of development which precedes "full development of the foundation of industrial society," refers to European feudalism. Between feudalism and capitalism there exists a fundamental connection: the former is the necessary precondition of the latter. But where in this schema can we fit non-European (nonfedual) patriarchy?

The theory of the Asiatic mode of production and the notion of "Oriental despotism" suggest an "Asiatic" or an "Oriental" social formation with a specific form of patriarchy. Marx, following Hegel, maintained that the history of classical antiquity was the history of cities founded on landed property and agriculture—unlike Eastern cities. In the Middle Ages the countryside rather than the city was the seat of history, whose development was propelled by the contradiction between town and countryside.[2] For Marx, the "Asiatic" city was not the same as the city of antiquity or the late Middle Ages; it was a specifically patriarchal phenomenon, in the Eastern sense of the term: a "royal camp" not a civil structure. But we are interested here in seeing whether it is possible to speak of a patriarchal form that is *neither* European nor Asiatic, as Marx has characterized these—one with its own peculiar history and structure, which can be identified as distinctively Arab (Islamic), not merely Asian or non-European.

When I speak of Arab patriarchy, I have in mind a specific psychosociological totality which is encountered in social and psychological structures. It is a system of values and social practices belonging to a determinate economy and culture. In this perspective the best way to grasp the meaning of patriarchy is to approach it from the standpoint of modernity, its historical successor and dialectical opposite.

Modernity

What is modernity? What does it mean to be modern? The table below points to possible answers by contrasting modernity with patriarchy in terms of a number of key categories.

Category	Modernity	Patriarchy
Knowledge	Thought/reason	Myth/belief
Truth	Scientific/ironic	Religious/allegorical
Language	Analytical	Rhetorical
Government	Democratic/socialist	Neopatriarchal sultanate
Social relations	Horizontal	Vertical
Social stratification	Class	Family/clan/sect[3]

Marshall Berman, in a seminal work on modernity, characterized it by reference to four basic aspects.[4] The first aspect is that modernity is a uniquely European phenomenon[5]—a fact which has had devastating existential consequences for the non-Western world. The second aspect concerns the historical content of modernity. This refers to the historical process which began in Europe, in the Renaissance and Reformation, with the collapse of the polarity, characteristic of traditional premodern thought, between a real world and an illusory one. Until then, the sensuous world had been viewed as illusory and the true world as accessible only through religion or philosophy, becoming available to human beings only in a future existence after death. The modern vision transformed this view as follows: "Now the false world is seen as a historical past, a world we have lost (or are in the process of losing), while the true world is in the physical and social world that exists for us here and now (or is in the process of coming into being)."[6]

The third aspect derives from Marx's analysis of the bourgeois revolution in the *Communist Manifesto:* in removing the veils of "religious and political illusion," the bourgeois revolution unmasked the reality of social relations and brought to light new options and new hopes. Berman: "Unlike the common people of all ages, who have been endlessly betrayed and broken by their devotion to the 'natural superiors,' modern people, 'washed in the icy water of egotistical calculation,' are free from deference to masters who destroy them, animated rather than numbed by the cold."[7] The possibility of genuine *rebellion* is a product of the new age. Because mod-

modernity ise fantasy

ern individuals "know how to think of, by, and for themselves, they will demand a clear account of what their bosses and rulers are doing for them—and doing to them—and be ready to resist and rebel where they are getting nothing in return."[8]

The fourth aspect concerns the character of the new bourgeois society that now comes into being, replacing and obliterating the old one: "a genuinely open society, not only economically but politically and culturally as well, so that people will be free to shop around and seek the best deals, in ideas, associations, laws and social policies, as well as in things."[9]

Thus, the dominant forces governing this modern society are different from those of every preceding type of society; they derive from its *secular* outlook and its *scientific* mode of thought.

Hegel, the first European thinker to address history as a central philosophical issue and to formulate a systematic way of thinking about it, based his position on an uncompromising idealistic dialectic; but revolutionary as his dialectic was philosophically, it could not carry his thought beyond the religious and political horizon of his time. Only with Marx and with late nineteenth-century German sociology (primarily Max Weber) do we have an interpretation of history and historical change based on concrete social and economic grounds.

The key notion associated with the rise of modern capitalism, for Marx, is its revolutionary character, for Weber, its distinctive rationality. Thus we can see modernity as simultaneously reason and revolution.

In Marx's view it was the bourgeois revolution which introduced the most dynamic features of modernity—constant agitation, movement, and change. As he put it in the *Manifesto,*

Constant revolutionizing of production, uninterrupted disturbance of all social conditions, everlasting uncertainty and agitation distinguish the bourgeois epoch from all earlier ones. All fixed, fast frozen relations, with their train of ancient and venerable prejudices and opinions, are swept away, all newformed ones become antiquated before they can ossify. All that is solid melts into air.[10]

For Weber also, modernity is an intrinsic part of capitalism.
Like Marx, he saw capitalism transforming European society
(and the world) in a radical, irreversible way. Unlike Marx,
he attributed this transformative force to "rationality"—instrumental reason calculating the relation between ends and
means. For Weber, rationality was the all-pervasive power
governing not only production but all spheres of bourgeois
life. Bureaucracy, and its "rationalization of all functions and
relations," was the process that was subjecting the whole world
to "disenchantment"—the metaphor of stripping as self-discov-
ery (Berman).[11] But Weber lacked Marx's optimism. While
Marx saw the crises of bourgeois society as ultimately leading
to revolutionary transcendence, Weber saw the power of un-
folding bureaucracy overwhelming human beings and society
and enclosing them in an "iron cage" from which there was
no escape—a vision deepened in our own day by the radical
skeptics of advanced industrial society (e.g., the post-structuralist writings of Foucault, Derrida, Deleuze, etc.).

So far we have used the term modernity to refer to a number of social phenomena and attitudes which still need to be
defined. A preliminary characterization of modernity may be
formulated in terms of its dynamics: *On the level of thought
modernity is dialectical, on the level of action it is revolutionary.*

Viewed historically against the broad context of European
experience from the end of the fifteenth to the twentieth century, modernity represents a coherent totality with clearly differentiated characteristics. Three characteristics stand out, enabling us to see modernity in three forms: as a comprehensive
structure, as a totalizing process, and as a determinate consciousness. I shall term these characteristics *modernity* (structure), *modernization* (process), and *modernism* (consciousness).[12]

Modernization, the process of economic and technological
transformation as it first occurred in Europe, represents a historical, uniquely European phenomenon. *Modernity,* under-

stood in terms of structure, consists of the host of elements and relations that together form the distinctive cultural whole we characterize as *modern;* modernity construed as consciousness is a *model* through which modern Europe recognized itself by differentiating itself from the (nonmodern) Other. *Modernism,* consciousness of being modern, is a vision involving the transformation of Self and the world,[13] which finds its expression not only in "reason" and "revolution," but in art, literature, and philosophy as well.

Modernity and *modernism*—the *structure,* and the *consciousness* appropriate to it—are grounded in the process of *modernization,* the dialectic of change and transformation.

Since Herodotus, people in the West always believed that civilization was something transmittable, like a gift or a disease. People became civilized through interaction, through learning one another's ways. In this view, civilization is the product of such interaction and transmission taking place over time among different peoples.

This construct might well be sufficient as a model to account for cultural change in traditional or premodern societies. But with the emergence of *modernity* a profound structural transformation sets in and a new stage of history begins. Cultural development is no longer a simple matter of borrowing and transmitting between cultural equals, but a relationship between a center of power and domination on the one side and a dependent and subordinate periphery on the other. It can be fairly said that neopatriarchal society was the outcome of modern Europe's colonization of the patriarchal Arab world, of the marriage of imperialism and patriarchy. I shall discuss this relationship in Chapter 4. In the rest of this chapter I shall focus on the question: In what sense is neopatriarchal society modernized?

"Modernization" and Patriarchy

The term "modernization," used here to denote "modern" *in a patriarchal context,* has as a central characteristic, crucial to the understanding of contemporary Arab neopatriarchy, that it refers to an *indigenous phenomenon resulting from contact with European modernity in the imperialist age.* "Modernization" is expressed in everyday material things—dress, food, life style; in institutions—schools, theaters, parliament; and in literature, philosophy, and science. The term refers to entities as well, such as a culture or society, or the subcultures and social subgroups that make it up; thus one may speak of a "modernized" culture or a "modernized" society, as well as "modernized" individuals, elites, strata, and so on. Obviously, the change denoted by "modernized" is in each case the outcome in one form or another of the influence of modernity on patriarchal practices and institutions. For this definition the central point is that being "modernized" signifies an *external* agency acting upon an internal development, thereby transforming it.[14] Whenever "modernization" sets in, internal, autonomous development is distorted, assuming the form of underdevelopment. The built-in distortion of "modernization" is due not merely to internal failure, but to something else. As we shall see this "something else" is in part the fact that the success of modernization itself is *disabling* when carried out in the framework of dependency and subordination and resulting in neopatriarchy.

This framework arose as a result of the disparate forms development took in Europe and in the periphery in modern times. Only in Europe, being the first to modernize, was the transformation into modernity (the process of modernization) autonomous and therefore authentic. In all the other cultures, with the exception of Japan, modernization occurred under dependent conditions, which led to distorted, inauthentic modernity—that is, to "modern" or "modernized" patriarchy, the neopatriarchy we encounter today.

It is important to note that in their development the various patriarchal societies were hampered not only by internal heteronomous structures, but also by the decisiveness with which Europe emerged as the center of wealth and power in the world. Europe's unique achievement consisted in its ability to transcend its *feudal* patriarchalism and to effect transition to modernity wholly on its own. The other leading cultures (Arab Islam, Hindu India, Buddhist China) were, by virtue of Europe's phenomenal breakthrough, caught in the global European-dominated system that followed upon this success. Thus, internal *heteronomy* and external *dependency* doomed these cultures to various forms of distorted modernized growth.

Manifest and Latent Structures

Neopatriarchal society, as "modernized," is essentially schizophrenic, for beneath the immediately encountered modern appearance there exists another latent reality. Between these two there is opposition, tension, contradiction. Analysis of this phenomenon will provide the key to understanding the dynamics and patterns of behavior characteristic of neopatriarchy, and will enable us to grasp a fundamental insight: *Patriarchal societies, regardless of their variety on the manifest level, all share in the same deep structures.*

From this perspective we can immediately grasp the curious aspect shared by all types of neopatriarchy, *the absence equally of genuine traditionalism and of authentic modernity*. In "modernized" patriarchy it is just as hard to find a truly modern individual or institution as it is to locate genuinely traditional ones. Indeed, both types are anomalous, whether in the conservative or in "progressive" countries of the Arab world. In neopatriarchal society (whether in its conservative or progressive segments or variants), the dominant type of individual is the "modernized." This is even more true today than a generation or two ago; for the most remote countries and countryside in the Arab world have in the last two or three decades been drawn into "modernity."

Since the Second World War, the subculture characterized by Hourani as Levantine, the prototypically "modernized" type,[15] has expanded rapidly as Europe has become more accessible and Western education more available, at least to the urban middle and upper strata. This development in turn has contributed to the growth of a socially important group, the "modernized" intellectuals,[16] the group in which the structural duality and contradictions of society are most clearly apparent. As we shall see, neopatriarchy has no stronger ally, and authentic modernity no more formidable foe, than this culturally schizophrenic group.

Model-Oriented Consciousness

The essential characteristic of "modernized" *consciousness*, by which I mean an intellectual disposition or a general orientation pattern, is its tendency to convert models into fetishes. We observe this trend in Arab society in the way, for example, education or dress or artistic production or even socialism are approached and appropriated as models and guides. Education, the manner of dress, socialist organization, and modernity itself are defined in terms of translations of Western models.

Fetishized consciousness exhibits two related and mutually reinforcing tendencies, *imitation* and *passivity*. Ideas, actions, values, or institutions are validated (or invalidated) not by criticism but by reference to a *model*. Fetishized modernism, a category which to a large extent determines neopatriarchal outlook and practice, imposes itself directly, without mediation or critical self-consciousness. It governs all kinds of activities, including creative ones, for example, "modern" Arabic poetry.[17] This holds true not only for "imported" ideas and institutions but also for ones that seem indigenous and self-generated. Take, for example, Arab nationalism, the central movement of Arab political life in the twentieth century. When examined from this perspective, Arab nationalism is impossible to conceive without reference to the European concept and experience (e.g., Japan's *autonomous* modernity cannot be understood without reference to the West). Politics, in the sense of both ideology and practice, is a reflection of European models.

As we shall later see (when we address modernization *theory*), the real difficulty with dependent, model-oriented consciousness has to do more with the modalities of thought than with its content. To be effective, the process of transforming consciousness must be grounded in *autonomy,* where patriarchy and its psychological relations have been grasped and overcome, or at least rendered no longer hegemonic.

Thus, by this definition, modernism, which in Europe is modernity's expression in art, literature, philosophy, and all forms of creative endeavor, becomes in neopatriarchy a reflected, fetishized practice, both dependent and noncritical. It is here that the false, distorted character of neopatriarchal "modernity" appears most clearly.

3

The Social Formation
of Neopatriarchy

Stages and Types of Patriarchy

As a social formation, patriarchy is a distinctive structure, the product of specific cultural and historical conditions. From the diachronic (historical) viewpoint, patriarchal social formation is a determinate succession of *stages;* from the synchronic (structural) standpoint, it is a series of interrelated *types*. Insofar as each type belongs to a corresponding stage, all types of patriarchal society are necessarily *transitional*—except perhaps for the contemporary type, neopatriarchy, which (like capitalism) is *terminal*, inasmuch as it marks the end of patriarchal society as such and the emergence of a qualitatively different type (modern society).[1]

What *stages* and *types* of Arab Islamic patriarchy can we identify from a diachronic/synchronic standpoint? The periods run as follows:

Pre-Islamic
Muhammad (and immediate successors)
Umayyad/Abbassid caliphate
Petty sultanates
Ottoman caliphate/sultanate
Neopatriarchy

The following types may be identified:

Pristine
Traditional
Premodern
"Modern"

(Note that the division between the last stage, "modern," and all the previous ones, parallels but is not fully identical with Weber's distinction between modern and traditional.) Our analysis focuses on the "modern" stage (which, as we have seen, is not truly modern and constitutes a last stage) and on the specific type of (patriarchal) social formation corresponding to it. The structural prototypes constitutive for *all* types of patriarchal social formations may preliminarily be identified as follows:

The pristine patriarchal family in the (nomadic or settled) tribal formation

The *tribalized* social formation

The *clan* (extended family) structure of the classical Islamic city

The family/clan in the context of *merchant capitalist relations*

At this juncture this question immediately presents itself: What characteristics of the patriarchal social formation have sustained and favored the persistence of its structural prototypes?

Basically there are two: the stubborn resistance of the tribal/clan type to structural change (from pre-Islamic times to the end of the nineteenth century); and the rise at a relatively early stage (seventh century) of a powerful ideological/legal system which served to reinforce the kinship system and to strengthen patriarchal relations within more advanced social and economic forms.[2]

The Tribal Bond

The tribal structure, the pristine type of patriarchal organization, has persisted in all types of patriarchal society up to and including the "modern" one. Tribalism is a basic characteristic without which it is impossible to account for the specific nature of Arab neopatriarchy.

The outstanding dynamic of the tribe-dominated structure is *factionalism*. As the term is used here, factionalism is a privative tendency; it first separates the Self from all Others, then, on a higher level, divides the world into opposing pairs— kin and non-kin, clan and opposing clan, Islam and non-Islam, and so forth. For it, affiliation based on blood ties supersedes every other kind of relation.

In its "modern" form tribalism takes on a subtler, less-pronounced expression, but its foundation is the same. It begins to weaken only with the beginning of the disintegration of the traditional economic structure—that is, with the capitalization of the economy speeded up by the coming of oil wealth and the consumer society, the rise of the nuclear family, and the dawning of radical supra-tribal consciousness. This process has just begun and is still subject to sudden arrest or reversal, as events in the 1970s and 1980s in Lebanon and across the Arab world have shown.

Factional ethics are simple and reductive. Within the tribal-dominated structure, obligations are strictly defined; outside it there are no clearly defined social obligations, except those contingently or contractually undertaken. Thus, in pristine patriarchy, "When you were at war with another tribe, it was a case of 'nothing barred.' The only restraints on your behavior towards an enemy or even a stranger were set by fear of retaliation or fear of supernatural power."[3] Tribal allegiance is not expressly ideological but rooted in basic needs.[4] The persistence of clan or sectarian allegiance in neopatriarchal society reveals how extensively modern patriarchy has been tied to primordial forms. Neither the city nor the society or state have succeeded in evolving social forms providing for genuine, alternative structures. Kinship and religious affiliation remain the ultimate ground of loyalty and allegiance, stronger than abstract ideology.

The essence of tribal practice is expressed in the individual's identification with the tribe, and this is reciprocated in the tribe's collective responsibility for the individual's actions, which in turn constantly renews and reinforces a person's kinship identification and loyalty.

The greatness of Muhammad's political achievement rests not so much in his success in dissolving tribal ties and overcoming tribal factionalism, but in the way he was able to fit existing social and psychological bonds into the structure of the new Islamic community. The Islamic *ummah* (nation) turned out to be nothing more than a supertribe, the projection of the universal tribal ethos. God, as Muhammad portrays Him, is a psychologically familiar figure. Submission, the basic relation of pristine patriarchy, here finds its most powerful ideological expression.

Again, let me note that these superstructural developments took place in a specific historical period under determinate social and physical conditions. We cannot comprehend the Muhammadan phenomenon without taking into account the higher forms of tribal organization that were objectively needed at this conjuncture (to which need Muhammad successfully responded) or the economic transformations then arising from the growth in long-distance trade, which required closer cooperation between the tribes and protection of communication routes. These needs and processes simultaneously favored Muhammad's movement and were presupposed by it.

Family and Tribe

What in the Arab Islamic tribal ethos gave pristine patriarchy its distinctive character?

Marx provides the most satisfying framework for attempting an answer. He saw the tribal structure taking form in two ways: under the impact of external factors, and as a result of internal developments. He saw the tribal group, once it settles down, becoming subject to various external conditions—"climatic, geographic, etc.,"—which "modify" it, that is, determine its mode of production. Then another, internal factor presents itself, which plays an equally important role in determining the development of the group, now a settled community. This factor determines the "particular natural predisposition" of the clan or the "clan character," as he calls it.[5] What is this clan character? What could it be but the product of the particular natural setting combined with the historical experience of the clan?

The building-block in the structure of the clan community is the family. To understand tribal structure—that is, the structure of patriarchal society as a whole—presupposes grasping the distinctive character of the Arab family.[6]

In its primordial form, the structure of the family is indistinguishable from that of the tribe. The tribe, as Marx put it, is simply "the family extended as a clan or through intermarriage between families, or combination of clans."[7] The emergence of the extended and nuclear family, as distinct from the clan family, represents a fairly recent development which is linked to urbanization and class stratification.

In a general way, the traditional kinship structure of patriarchal society may be differentiated according to the socioeconomic setting:

Urban
Village
Bedouin (sedentary or semi-settled)

Family identification may occur according to a fourfold differentiation:

Tribe (*qabilah*)

Subtribe (*'ashirah*)

Clan or lineage (*hamulah*)

Extended family (*'ailah*)

The nuclear family (*usrah*) has been slow in emerging and restricted in most cases to the upper and middle urban strata. Urban mass society represents an extension of the countryside and as such is dominated by the kinship system of village and tribe. By its constitution patriarchal society favors the prevalence of the extended (patriarchal) family and the restriction of the nuclear (democratic) family. To the extent that the latter family form is allowed to spread and develop, patriarchal power suffers and is forced to retreat. In this sense, the prevalence of the nuclear family, and the values on which it is based, represents the most serious structural threat to the existing neopatriarchal formation.

This becomes clearer when we consider the implications of the nuclear family structure for patriarchal hegemony. There are three basic considerations in this regard. First, the *economic* consideration: the nuclear family is both an outcome and a motivating force of economic transformation. Here I refer not merely to the bourgeoisification of urban society, but specifically to the erosion of traditional vertical relations. In a household where the children have received a degree of education and acquired specific skills, they have by the same token gained independence and mobility. The children are no longer dependent on the father as in a rural or precapitalist setting. The father now finds himself forced into a new relationship within the household and with each of its members.

This brings us to our second consideration, which has to do with *democratic* relations. If the essential relation of patriarchy is subordination, that of the nuclear family is equality. Economic independence is the basis of the nuclear family's democracy, the condition for the overthrow of patriarchal

tyranny. Thus it may be said that, formally, the end of patriarchal hegemony depends on the disintegration of the extended clan family and the prevalence of the nuclear democratic family.

The third consideration centers on the *emancipation of
women*. In the transition from the patriarchal to the modern
family, women are certainly the primary beneficiaries. Famil-
ial patriarchy provides the ground for a dual domination—of
the father over the family household, and of the male over
the female. In itself, the structure of the modern family provides the necessary (but not *sufficient*) ground for the liberation of women. The precondition is access to education and
to work and thus to economic independence.

Women and Neopatriarchy

Now let me attempt a closer characterization of women's place
in the patriarchal structure of Arab society and the family.
Two Arab women writers have for the first time laid bare the
situation, which neopatriarchal writers have surreptitiously
covered up and Islamic reformists have systematically mysti-
fied. Nawal al-Sadawi, an Egyptian psychiatrist, fearlessly embarked, in her book *Woman and Sexuality*,[8] on a total confrontation, raising not only the social and economic aspects of
women's liberation but the sexual as well. And in *Beyond the
Veil* Fatima Mernissi, a Moroccan sociologist,[9] raised, besides
the question of sexuality, the legal-judicial aspect of woman's
subordination and the ways it might be changed in a truly
modern Muslim society.

Until the appearance of these two books, these problems
were dealt with from mainly two perspectives, the conservative and the reformist.[10] The reformists, since the turn of the
century, genuinely sought to focus on some of the major issues
connected with the degraded position of women in society,
but they did not address the central problems, which were
intertwined with religious and legal issues, and never went

beyond a vague notion of "renewal" (*tajdid*). As for the conservatives, their position consisted essentially in rationalizing the status quo and opposing structural change. Both reformists and conservatives reflected in their discourse the dominant ideology of neopatriarchal society: a conservative, relentless male-oriented ideology, which tended to assign privilege and power to the male at the expense of the female, keeping the latter under crippling legal and social constraints. The formulations of Sadawi and Mernissi appear so radical because they deal head-on with the specific implications of these constraints. Neopatriarchy, inwardly preoccupied with sex and outwardly behaving as though sex did not exist, here suffers merciless exposure and ridicule.

It is difficult to explain to the non-Arab reader the effect the following passage can have on the Arab Muslim male.

Sadawi:

> Men think that the vagina . . . is the woman's most sensitive organ, and that the slightest contact with the male brings about the woman's orgasm. From here stems the myth that the size of the man's organ is the decisive factor for the male's sexual prowess, and that the sexually capable man is the one with the biggest or the longest organ.
>
> In fact the clitoris and the penis are similar in shape and structure and have the same sensitivity and importance in the sexual act. This is not amazing or strange, for the two organs have the same origin in both sexes: the cells that make up the clitoris also make up the penis. But what happens in the early evolution of the fetus is that the feminine clitoris ceases to develop at a given stage while the male organ continues to grow for a long period of time.[11]

Mernissi touches on the same issue in somewhat different but equally defiant terms.

> The Muslim system is not so much opposed to women as to the heterosexual unit. What is feared is the growth of the involvement between a man and a woman into an all-encompassing love, satisfying the sexual, emotional, and intellectual needs of both partners. Such an involvement constitutes a direct threat to the man's alle-

giance to Allah, which should be the unconditional investment of all man's energies, thought, and feelings in his God.[12]

Both Sadawi and Mernissi take a rational, systematic approach drastically different from the rhetorical, superficial approach of the reformists and traditionalists. These two feminist writers adhere to different analytical frameworks, Sadawi leaning toward a psychoanalytical and Marxist approach and Mernissi to Western social science, yet they agree on the fundamental preconditions of liberation: radical social change and the overthrow of patriarchal hegemony. Neither defines the essentially political character of the solution but both see socialism as the answer to the problems of both social injustice and the oppression of women. They are, however, equally aware of the pitfalls involved. Sadawi writes:

> Women should know that true socialism, that is, justice and equality among human beings, does not become reality merely by raising socialist slogans, or merely by legislating socialist laws. Changing the laws is necessary, but in itself is not enough to bring about change.[13]

Change will only come by changing the *relation* between male and female in society, in social practice—a long-term process involving "new modes of upbringing, based on complete equality between men and women in all the stages of life, from birth to death, an equality in rights and duties inside the home and outside it and in the education of children.[14]

Mernissi quotes the Marxist Syrian writer George Tarabishi's declaration that the Arabs are not a hundred million people but only fifty million, the female population being a paralyzed half.[15] Furthermore, she considers Muslim-Arab patriarchal society as a male-constituted society.

> The whole system was so organized as to allow the males in society to dispose of the female half of the population as they would of their other possessions. . . . Palliatives are not enough. Society *cannot* afford to be merely reformist, where women's liberation and social justice are concerned.[16]

Patriarchy and Nationalist Consciousness

Two main issues—one concerning social structure, the other regarding consciousness—are involved in a consideration of patriarchy and nationalism. I shall here briefly treat these issues from the standpoint of their interconnection.

Patriarchal society, in its traditional as well as its modern form, derives its strength from its ability to satisfy *basic* needs. Humanity's primary social structures—the family, the clan, the religious sect—are those which most successfully address its most fundamental needs: material interests, security, identity.[17]

In neopatriarchal society, a person is lost when cut off from the family, the clan, or the religious group. The state cannot replace these protective primary structures. Indeed, the state is an alien force that oppresses one, as is equally civil society, a jungle where only the rich and powerful are respected and recognized. In one's *actual* practice one conducts oneself *morally* only within the primary structures (family-clan-sect); for the most part, one lives amorally "in the jungle," in the society at large. In this duality is reflected the fundamental division in Muslim ideology between an external world of conflict outside the boundaries of the community (*dar al-Harb*) and a world of peace and harmony (*dar al-Islam*) existing within it.[18] This ideology fails to recognize that for the mass of the people the realm of struggle and strife exists not outside society but at its very heart.

The traditional Japanese family, for example, instills solidarity and obedience in its young as conditions of survival just as the Arab family does; but whereas those values are carried over by the Japanese outside the family into the larger society, in Arab society they tend to remain confined within the micro groups. Similarly, in China, Maoism effected the transition from family loyalty to collective loyalty not by radical transformation of the values that obtained within the fam-

ily but by "a substitution that retains the style of piety while
providing new objects to be loved and cherished." For example, the duty of children to "serve the parents" is supplanted
by the duty of children to "serve the people." To be sure, the
ideal of supplanting values (e.g., "love of country above love
of self")[19] is universally extolled by Arab nationalism but
never institutionalized in structures that would insure its
translation into actual behavior.

Thus nationalist consciousness (the sense of distinctive national identity) could never take root on a mass level in neopatriarchy; the contradiction between the primary structures
and the modern structures, corrupted by the power and wealth
of the narrowly based ruling elites, will continue to obstruct
such a possibility. National *feeling* derives not from secular
ideology advocated by the intellectual elite, but from religious
consciousness instilled by the clerics and sectarian leaders.
Similarly, failure to respond to the nationalist call (to rise
against the foreign occupier) is rooted in the priorities defined
by family loyalty and sectarian interests.

For mass consciousness, the category *nation* may not very
easily be differentiated from the (religious) category *ummah,*
nor nationalist doctrine fully separated from religious identity. The reason for this is simple: as long as the relations of
status, power, and wealth typical of neopatriarchal society remain essentially unchanged, the ideological categories dominating mass consciousness are not likely to change in a radical
fashion. And no matter how "modern" neopatriarchal society
might become, the popular mass will continue to reject secular nationalism in practice and to adhere to religious identity.
Consciousness will continue to be tied to the concrete relations of the social reality.

National consciousness is frustrated by another factor,
equally difficult to surmount in the absence of fundamental
political change: the contradiction between the fundamental
presupposition of Arab nationalism (one united Arab nation)
and the *reality* of neopatriarchal society (multiple sovereign

Arab nation-states). As long as the nationalist vision was sustained by concrete struggle against foreign domination (Ottoman or colonial) or Arab unitary praxis (Nasserism), the nationalist project still represented the principal possibility for breaking up neopatriarchal society and paving the way to the transformation of its basic relations. But with independence, patriarchalism gained a decisive victory over secular nationalism. Independence led not to national unity but to multistate neopatriarchy; patriarchalism not only withstood the unitary wave of the 1950s and 1960s but succeeded in becoming the consecrator of the nation-state system, investing it with the legitimacy of sovereignty.

In the age of oil wealth nationalist consciousness, confronting on one hand the gravitational pull of family and kin and on the other the alienating push of the neopatriarchal nation-state, experienced the most serious setback since its inception. As a result, in the last quarter of the twentieth century Arab nationalism has begun to lose its momentum. The relations and values of neopatriarchy have gained the ascendancy (1970s and 1980s), and Islamic fundamentalism has moved to the center of the political stage. Fundamentalist Islamic thought, which with its absolutist simplicity gives its movement a popular depth and intensity which secularist Arabism never enjoyed, has now superseded the ambivalence inherent in Arab nationalist consciousness. Indeed, militant Islamic fundamentalism as a form of political consciousness has now made possible the emergence of the first genuine mass movement the Arab world has seen since the Kharijite movement (seventh century). Thus modern patriarchalism, by its tendency to suppress secular nationalism and free political development, may have finally unleashed the revolutionary potential of patriarchal fundamentalism, thereby letting loose the forces of its own negation (a development we shall discuss in Chapter 9).

One last question must be raised—that concerning the relation of patriarchy to class consciousness. This question may be dealt with on two levels: we might seek to characterize the *content* of consciousness; or we might try to identify its *social locus*.

The major difficulty, from the theoretical or the practical point of view, is identifying the specific *class* to which a consciousness belongs. Correct as class analysis might be, it does not altogether dispose of the essential difficulty of identifying a *class* in a neopatriarchal context. Nor, in this case, is analogical discussion of Third World countries (Vietnam, China, Cuba), where the analysis of class is often subordinated to the needs of social praxis, adequate for grasping the cultural and economic specificity of Arab neopatriarchal society. It is perhaps useful every now and then to glance at the map of the Arab world in order to remind ourselves of its location, structure, and peculiar geography; and to recall that until well into the nineteenth century it largely consisted of fragmented and isolated groupings of decayed cities, stagnant villages, impoverished peasantry, and marauding bedouin.

But contemporary neopatriarchal Arab society is *new*. And its distinctive character is reflected in the newness of its social composition, which is in a state of formation and flux. At this moment we witness the emergence within it of the new composite class I referred to earlier, scattered in contrasting urban and rural settings, forming an undifferentiated popular mass, which is increasingly polarized to a small hegemonic elite. Its consciousness is still patriarchal, governed by categories not of "class" or "nation" but of inherited faith and traditional value, with their potential for both *acquiescence* and *militancy*. Yet mobilization, even under the banner of patriarchal fundamentalist ideology, may have the potential of radicalizing this group in the direction of some kind of class consciousness.

To conclude, then, the analysis of "modern" neopatriarchal society as it presents itself today in the Arab world, whether as "progressive" or conservative, typically does not yet allow as its central analytical category class (a potential "for-itself"), but only the category mass, the totality encompassing the subtotalities of family, clan, sect, or religion. Thus, from this view, the question of *national* or *class* consciousness is not one of identifying the social subject to whom those types of consciousness properly belong, but of deciding whether the traditional petty bourgeois/proletarian mass (armed with fundamentalist consciousness) might not, by its spontaneous action, eventually achieve what the nationalists and secular radicals failed to accomplish—namely, the dissolution and displacement of contemporary neopatriarchal society.

4

The Structure and
Relations of Neopatriarchy

A basic thesis of this study proceeds from the assumption that the category *class* by itself is not sufficient for a proper grasp of the essential character of neopatriarchalism. We need a perspective from which we can at once glimpse the historical, developmental aspect of neopatriarchal society as well as its inner dynamics.

According to Marx, the impulse to development is the maturation of humanity's productive powers (forces of production). And when he speaks of development he has in mind a broad evolutionary process. This concept, while indispensable for accounting for social change over the long duration, overshoots the narrower spaces of single epochs and specific events that compose the broad movement of history. Only in this narrower context does the cultural specificity of particular societies come into view and lend itself to closer analysis. A narrower perspective also endows superstructural elements with explanatory value; social reality, when made more specifically determinate, appears in its full concreteness and complexity. Critical analysis has to accommodate itself to this narrower approach by addressing a wider range of sociopsychological phenomena and by borrowing from the language and categories of other disciplines.

Authority and Submission

Our discussion has never assumed that neopatriarchy has a permanent, universal nature or character, but has rather referred to a dynamic structure approached from the standpoint of types and stages, the moments of its sociohistorical development. Now we will approach it in terms of its inner structure, whose essential core and building block is the patriarchal family, historically the origin and model of neopatriarchal society.

The patriarchal family's significance for understanding neopatriarchal structures lies in its basic internal relations, above all in the relations of *authority, domination,* and *dependency,* which both reflect and are reflected in the structure of social relations.[1]

The Lebanese social psychologist Ali Zay'our, in his analysis of the patriarchal family in Arab society,[2] approaches the problem from the standpoint of the production of personality. His central thesis focuses on the "lostness" of the individual in the father-dominated family and the neopatriarchally organized society, and the denial by both of the possibility of "self-fulfillment."[3]

> The family is relentless in its repression. [The child] is brought up to become an obedient youth, subservient to those above him—his father, older brother, clan chief, president.[4]

The father, the prototypical neopatriarchal figure, is the central agent of repression.[5] His power and influence are "grounded in punishment."[6]

> The main concern is that the child be obedient, well-mannered, ignorant about sexual matters, "better" than his fellows. . . . By being compared to others to underscore his failure he is driven to view himself negatively and to lose self-esteem (to the extent of self-punishment at times).[7]

Zay'our links repression in the family to the prevalence of "irrational and superstitious" attitudes in the mass of the population, which facilitates control by the status quo and makes people blindly opposed to social change. He sees this as a structural aspect of the existing society.

> The scientific mind, which explains phenomena by reference to causes that are subject to examination and verification, has not taken root in the collective personality. The magical, supernatural orientation is still dominant and is active in the psychic structure of the individual. Thus, rationality is not the governing principle of individual behavior or of social action in general. There are [in society] two sectors existing next to one another, one magical, the other scientific; traditional structures coexist alongside modern structures, a primitive, dependent economy alongside a rational modern economy.[8]

Zay'our is aware that the malaise is caused by specific historical and social factors which, if understood, could be confronted and transformed.[9] He also knows that the personality traits he analyzes are the product not of an essential "nature" but of social conditions that could be changed. He insists on the need for critical self-knowledge, a process to which he contributes by his analysis, as the precondition for possessing the appropriate consciousness.

> How are we to criticize [distorted Western] views about us and to oppose and combat them if we remain—as these theories maintain— naturally submissive, speculative, mythical?[10]

Zay'our assumes, as do Sadawi and Mernissi, the social origin of the self. By this he refers not merely to the emergence of the individual in the process of social evolution, but also to the social constitution of selfhood, an aspect which received its most systematic treatment by the Marxist psychoanalyst, Wilhelm Reich.[11]

From this vantage point we can glimpse how the socialization process may affect not only the "education" of the individual, but how it may condition one's inner capacity for perception and one's experience of oneself and others. It is precisely the interpretation of this process, as it unfolds within the family in neopatriarchal society, that Zay'our, Sadawi, Mernissi, and others have sought to achieve in their analyses.

Implicit in this analysis is the assumption, fundamental to both the Marxist and Freudian perspectives, that deep structures in society and in the individual "act" independently of the consciousness of individuals and groups. Without this perspective it would be impossible to go beyond surface events and make intelligible the meaning of underlying structures. Central to our analysis are the deep structures of heteronomy and autonomy.

Heteronomy and Autonomy

As systems of value and social organization, heteronomy is based on subordination and obedience and upholds an ethic of authority, and autonomy is based on mutual respect and justice and adheres to an ethic of freedom.

The Swiss psychologist Jean Piaget has analyzed the tensions, and their consequences, emanating from the dialectic within these systems.[12]

According to Piaget, the system of obedience and subordination is revealed by the effective reactions of children before the age of seven or eight to the moral judgment and pronouncements of parents and grown-ups. Children at this age accept orders from parents and their surrogates so long as the one who gives them is *physically* present; in that person's absence the law loses its effectiveness and its violation causes only minor uneasiness. At a later stage, after the age of eleven or twelve, this power becomes permanent, as the child internalizes and identifies with the parental image or authority figures. But the submission that now occurs is not complete. The attitude toward the parents or authority figures is *ambivalent*. The child accepts orders from a superior, not just from anyone (peers or younger children). This acceptance is based on *respect*, which combines affection *and* fear.

This form of respect Piaget calls *unilateral*, "since it binds an inferior to a superior who is regarded as such." It is to be distinguished from mutual respect, which is founded on reciprocal esteem. Unilateral respect generates in the child an ethic of obedience, which is characterized by subordination to another's will.[13] Mutual respect, on the other hand, creates in the child an ethic, in a sense, of freedom, equality, and justice.

Normally as children move from one stage of development to another they achieve passage from a state of heteronomy to a state of autonomy. Piaget gives two examples of how this takes place. First, in games with rules, children before the age of seven receive the rules "ready-made from their elders (by a mechanism derived from unilateral respect) [and] regard them as 'sacred,' untouchable, and of transcendent origin (parents, the government, God, etc.)." Older children, however, have a different attitude toward these same rules. They regard them "as the result of an agreement among contemporaries, and accept the idea that rules can be changed by means of democratically arrived at consensus."[14]

Second, increasingly after the age of eight, *mutual respect and reciprocity* lead to the prevalence of *justice* over *obedience* as a central norm, "equivalent in the affective realm to the norm of coherence in the realm of cognitive operations."[15]

Piaget points out that an essential aspect of autonomy is that it leads more surely to respect for rules than heteronomy, where the physical absence of authority causes a breakdown of obedience. The child at this early stage of transformation begins to distinguish between "lawless whims" and "constitutional innovation." Thus under relations of equality

everything is allowed, every individual proposition is, by rights, worthy of attention. . . . To desire to change the laws is no longer sin against them. . . . No one has the right to introduce an innovation except by legal channels, i.e., by previously persuading the other players and by submitting in advance to the verdict of the majority. There may therefore be breaches but they are of procedure only: procedure alone is obligatory, opinion can always be subjected to discussion.[16]

By the fact that the child adheres to certain rules of discussion and cooperates with colleagues in full reciprocity, the child will be able to differentiate between "custom" and the "rational ideal" and so achieve the transition from heteronomy to autonomy.[17]

The point I wish to underscore is that the transition seems never complete in the Arab neopatriarchal family; this family continues to nurture the values and attitudes of heteronomy. The words of Wilhelm Reich summarize the social significance of this problem.

> It creates the individual who is forever afraid of life and of authority and thus creates again and again the possibility that masses of people can be governed by a handful of powerful individuals.[18]

The Patronage System

The neopatriarchal family, in producing the heteronomous individual, fulfills a basic need of neopatriarchal society: it reinforces the central system of patronage and assures the perpetuation of the primordial patriarchal authority.

Despite all ideological appearances, the individual's basic affiliation in "modernized," neopatriarchal society is to the family, the clan, the ethnic or religious group. For the common person in this society the concept of society or fatherland is an abstraction which has meaning only when reduced to the primordial significations of kinship and religion. In social practice the authority of father, tribal head, and religious leader (rather than considerations of nation or class) determines the direction and object of individual allegiance. This practice strengthens both personal loyalty and dependence, cultivated early within the family, and bolsters them within the larger social whole in the system of patronage and the distribution of favor and protection.

The lubricant of the patronage system endowing it with suppleness and resilience, is the *wasta* (mediation) mechanism.

The complex patronage system as it still exists today would not be so firmly rooted and difficult to dislodge were it not for this built-in mediating mechanism which, as it secures the protection and material interests of the individual and the group, including the lowest member of the group, strengthens the latter's sense of identity and cohesion. *Wasta,* in the form developed within the family, not only socializes the individual into accepting the supremacy of established authority but also trains one in the ways of dealing with it. Through the intercession of the mother, the uncle, a respected figure close to the family, and so forth, the child discovers that despite one's impotence one can still operate in the existing system of power. The larger social entity reflects this capacity: even the lowliest individual can gain a hearing at the centers of wealth and power, through the intercession of relatives or friends, or friends of relatives or friends of friends. Patronage, and the satisfaction of needs that goes with it, makes it easier for the individual to accept his or her condition. Although alienation is not wholly overcome, one has the sense of belonging in a system which affords one protection and bestows upon one an occasional favor.

What is unique about the patronage system is that everyone involved in it stands to gain. This becomes clear in the *wasta* mechanism, where the supplicant, the bestower of favor, and the go-between as well all get something. Still, the one who stands to gain most is the bestower of favor, the one who *has* the power and the wealth, enabling one to be generous.

For to beg at the doors of the powerful and the wealthy is often a matter of survival, a necessity forced upon the supplicant by social conditions one cannot change and to which one must submit. If one seeks refuge in the state and its laws, one soon discovers that these can provide one with neither justice nor protection. Neopatriarchal patronage, as it displaces legality and renders public institutions superfluous, takes away the individuals's claim to autonomous right.

An extreme case, which will illuminate this social syndrome, is the penalty which usually redounds upon the son for violating the father's will in the traditional household: he is reduced to impotence, he has no rights, owns nothing, and is totally at his father's mercy. All his effort is channeled toward finding ways of obtaining his father's forgiveness and good will. He learns by painful experience that he can hope to achieve his goal only by submitting to his father's will. At this point, he is granted some of his rights, as an adult which, in this context, he experiences as something not inherently possessed but bestowed from above.

Clearly, in the context of patronage based on impotence and submission, the concept of social contract is inconceivable. Society in actuality is only subject to the will of the rich and powerful, a will delimited only by material capacity and institutionalized ethical injunction. The law serves not the society but the established sociopolitical order; *crime* is not distinguished from *sacrilege* or *rebellion;* and punishment is intended not to reform but to restore the sanctity of the law and to safeguard existing social relations. Thus as legal opposition is not possible, conspiracy and rebellion become the only possible avenues of action. Similarly, when open discussion is disallowed the remaining form of persuasion is conspiracy and violence.

However, patronage inevitably renders inefficient any structure it dominates. In putting conformity above originality and obedience before autonomy, it crushes creative talent and encourages only those powers that help to maintain it. Its own interests and requirements, rather than those of the institution or social group it inhabits, become the final determinants of evaluation and action. This influence applies to universities, schools, hospitals, government agencies, and professional societies as well as the military establishment, the state bureaucracy, and the "revolutionary" party. No amount of external criticism can change the inner structure of the patronage system, for wherever patriarchal relations exist—subordination-domination, superiority-inferiority, loyalty-conformity—patronage *dominates*.

The irrationality of the neopatriarchal system is an innate characteristic not of patriarchy as such but, to repeat, of "modernized" patriarchy. In itself traditional patriarchal culture, with its systems of protection and coercion, generosity and obedience, is a derivative of conditions which no longer obtain. Traditional patriarchy, in its pure form, cannot survive in the modern world, not because it is "traditional" but because it is no longer so. And "modernized" patriarchy (neopatriarchy) is the vehicle of patriarchal society's continuing attempt to keep modernity at bay.

5

The Sociohistorical
Origins of Neopatriarchy

Here we ought to pause for a brief overview of the sociohistorical development of (neo)patriarchy. Central among the considerations we will raise is the question of feudalism, which, according to Samir Amin, is the kind of social formation that did *not* arise in the Arab world until the late nineteenth century, and then only as a result of European imperialism.[1] Perhaps of equal importance is the problem of institutional-legal modernization under the Ottomans in the nineteenth century, which led to the transformation of property ownership and the formation of a big landlord class. Politically, the crucial development is that involving the new ideological consciousness centered on social and political change, as reflected in secular liberalism and Islamic reformism. The final topic deserving our attention is the emergence in a modern form of the petty sultanate—small nation-state—as the dominant form of state power following national independence.

Political Forms of Traditional Patriarchy

Historically, the Arab world has seen the development of several types of political authority (and organization). As we have seen in Chapter 2, the most fundamental, because at the basis of all subsequent types, was the pristine or pre-Islamic type of authority, followed by the Islamic patriarchal type of Muhammad and the orthodox caliphs. Then came the Ummayyad and Abbassid *imperial caliphate* (seventh-thirteenth centuries), which gave the patriarchal type of government the form of universal state. The *sultanate,* the type which followed the dissolution of the imperial caliphate, first took the form of *petty state absolutism* and then, under the Ottomans, a new imperial *caliphate-sultanate* form, which endured until the twentieth century. All six types were conditioned by specific historical developments; the most important of these are: the early disintegration of imperial power (under the Ummayyads and Abbassids); the rapid fragmentation of the Muslim Arab world; the dominance of warrior elites and the rise of the petty sultanates (from the twelfth century); foreign invasions—the Seljuk, the Crusader, the Mongol, the Ottoman Turk; the collapse of long-distance trade (sixteenth century), followed by economic stagnation; the introduction of the Ottoman *tanzimat* (nineteenth-century modernization); and European economic and political hegemony, followed by direct European imperialism and colonialism.

Patriarchalism, in its early tribal form as well as in its politically more advanced forms under the empire and the sultanate, lacked a clear basis of territoriality. Its social basis was always religious-ethnic identity. So before the twentieth century Arab society actually saw only two social-political movements which involved the transcendence of family-clan identity and outlook, namely the Muhammadan revolution in the sixth century, which sought to replace tribal kinship with the universal community (*ummah*) of Islam; and the Arab nationalist movement, which sought to bind twentieth-century Arabs to a secular ideology within a single territorial fatherland.

But tribal patriarchalism from the very beginning proved internally resistant to change and remained a basic constitutive structure of the *ummah,* in both the religious and secular meanings of the term. Indeed, in the first instance, the tribal structure, far from dissolving, provided the ready-made framework of Muhammad's movement. The Islamic community consisted of Islamicized family-clans, so that, paradoxically, the narrowest mode of identity now served as the cornerstone of the structure of universal brotherhood. In the second instance, the secular meaning of the term *ummah* (nation) as intended by Arab nationalism—to denote territoriality as national identity—included both the Islamic and tribal components, a fact which perhaps accounts for the ambivalence at the heart of this movement.

Feudalism and the Patriarchal Order

In its socioeconomic development, the patriarchal structure was grounded in a tribal and mercantile formation distinguished by long-distance trade rather than purely peasant production. This formation crystallized into what Samir Amin termed, following Marx's discussion in the *Grundrisse*,[2] a "tributary and nonfeudal" mode of production.[3] According to this view landlordism, and with it a kind of feudalism, emerged in the Arab world only much later, when the Middle East had been integrated into the capitalist world market and fallen under direct colonial domination. This theory, though still somewhat speculative and in need of more empirical research, sheds some light on the distinctive development of Arab patriarchy. It raises the central question: In what way did European feudalism differ in its development from Arab patriarchal, tribute-paying society, and with what consequences?

The distinctive elements of Europe's social and economic development from the Renaissance down to modern times derive from its feudal heritage and experience. Feudalism as a social and economic formation represented a higher, more developed form of premodern patriarchy precisely because it was able to transcend the kinship system.[4] In European feudal society, social ties that had developed as blood ties *alone* proved no longer sufficient, while in Arab patriarchal society blood ties remained the basic social bonds, with the family-clan structure providing the fundamental unit of social relations. And whereas feudalism in western Europe was directly responsible for simultaneously creating local sovereignties and autonomous centers of rural production, in the Arab world towns never developed into independent juridical centers and were always separated from and dominated rural production. Urban centers were permanently polarized to the countryside. A social and judicial conception of an urban citizenry, based on feudal relations, as arose in Europe, never emerged in the kinship-based, tribally oriented cities and towns of Arab patriarchal society.

Yet, interestingly enough, medieval Arab patriarchy and medieval European feudalism were both based on an *unequal* rather than simply a *hierarchical* form of society. European knights and serfs represented roughly the same division of labor existing in the Arab world between the "warrior merchants," as Amin named them (following Max Weber),[5] and the immediate producers of the countryside.

The basic difference between the feudal and patriarchal models of authority lies in the way authority was articulated in each system. Marc Bloch saw feudalism's lasting contributions to Europe's political development expressed in the idea of *contractual* agreement between ruler and subjects. He concluded his great book on feudal society with these words:

> The originality [of Western feudalism] consisted in the emphasis it placed on the idea of an agreement capable of binding the rulers; and in this way, oppressive as it may have been to the poor, it has in truth bequeathed to our Western civilization something with which we still desire to live.[6]

In contrast, the concept of contract between ruler and ruled had no basis in either the theory or practice of Muslim Arab patriarchy. The will of the ruler was inherently unfettered, conditioned only by the will of God, which is to say its legitimacy derived from divine right rather than the consent of those it affected. Thus the juridical dictum, to obey the ruler though he be unjust, is mandatory; and rebellion may under no circumstances be justified. Of course, in practice this principle has almost always been violated; divisiveness and revolt have characterized every phase of Islamic history since the death of the Prophet. Yet theory has succeeded in maintaining a stubborn indifference to practice, so that opposition between what *is* and what *ought to be* could never allow the evolution of a real solution within its framework. In social practice this antagonism could find expression only in two opposite forms: total *submission* or *revolt*.

The Development of Precapitalist Patriarchy

At the time when Europe was entering its modern age and in the process of becoming the dominant center of world power, the Arab world was falling under the domination of the Ottoman sultanate and entering its period of decline (*inhitat*), which lasted well into the nineteenth century. Thus, the Ottoman period is decisive for the development of Arab neopatriarchy as we know it today.

In its basic structure at the time of its greatest expansion (sixteenth and seventeenth centuries), the Ottoman Empire represented a simple despotism. Montesquieu characterized it as "government where no man is a citizen."[7]

As mentioned earlier, during the four centuries of Ottoman rule the economy of the Arab world continued in steady decline as Europe gained power and primacy. By the end of the sixteenth century long-distance trade had suffered an irreversible setback, partly in consequence of the opening up of the sea routes around the Cape, and partly because production in the Arab economy, confined to agriculture and artisanal crafts, underwent no change in method or technique like that in Europe.

Until the nineteenth century there were, strictly speaking, no legal-rational regulations governing economic activity in the Ottoman Empire. In economic exchange Islamic law (Shari'a) provided the only ground for economic dealing, which tended ultimately to rest more on "moral" trust or physical intimidation than on legal regulation. Throughout most of this period the state often harassed the mercantile class and occasionally threatened it with arbitrary confiscations and brutal persecution. This situation hampered investment in large-scale enterprises and led to hoarding of gold and, later, the purchase of landed property rather than the accumulation of capital. A rational capitalist mode had little chance of arising alongside merchant capital.

Until the promulgation of the 1858 Land Code there were no private large-scale holdings in the Ottoman Empire and Egypt, except the sultan's (i.e., the state's). Urban private property was confined to households and religious foundations (*waqf*). And in the countryside, land ownership was determined by land use and tribute payment traditions rather than any form of legal title. A decade later (1867) an agrarian law was passed which for the first time gave local landowners juridical title to their estates.[8]

Amin's thesis, that a kind of feudalism emerged under the influence and pressure of nineteenth-century European imperialism, gains some credibility when seen in the light of these developments. Forms of landlordism had been implanted in the past: whenever nomadism gave way to settled agricultural activity, tribal patriarchy found expression in landholding, with the tribal chiefs disposing of privileged possessions. This process was going on long before the Ottoman conquest, and continued in certain parts of the Arab world into the nineteenth and twentieth centuries. But not until the promulgation of Western property laws did private landholding gain legal expression. And then a class of urbanized tribal chiefs, not a feudal landed aristocracy, came into being, and the new property laws consolidated their landed property and position—along with that of the big urban merchants-usurers, high government officials, and heads of notable families. Of all these it was distinctly the tribal chiefs who gained most, when they suddenly found themselves legal owners of large landholdings, much of which had been collectively held by the members of the tribe (peasants).

These legal-economic transformations imbued the precapitalist patriarchal structures with new political power. Without question, the establishment of colonial (and semi-colonial) rule at the end of the nineteenth and the early part of the twentieth centuries strengthened the position of the tribal chiefs, the traditional merchant families, and the religious and administrative notables, and endowed them with new social status, contributing to the emergence by the mid-twentieth century, when national independence was achieved, of a fairly clear-cut national bourgeoisie. Thus there is no doubt that European intervention in the Arab world had among its consequences *the juridical modernization of patriarchal structures in society.*

Ottoman Modernization

It will be recalled that Europe's head-on encounter with the Arab world, after the Crusades, took place first at the end of the eighteenth (Napoleon in Egypt) and then throughout the nineteenth and early twentieth centuries. When the French armies landed in Egypt in 1798, Arab society under Ottoman rule had declined to a state of almost complete dissolution. The economy had been reduced to the level of subsistence; the countryside was ravaged by nomadic incursions and the forays of soldiers and tax collectors; the towns were in decay, with hardly any commercial trade and only limited petty production (artisanal crafts); and the population, impoverished and illiterate, at the mercy of the sultan's governors, warlords, and mercenary soldiers, had little education or culture—science, philosophy, political theory, or self-conscious history. In addition, society lacked autonomous municipal organization and the benefit of any kind of civil autonomy.[9]

From this encounter emerged the first attempts at modernization by the Ottoman Empire and Egypt—first of the military
and bureaucratic structures, then the legal system, and later
education, the economy, and the modes of everyday life among
the privileged social groups. It can be said that the disintegration of the Ottoman economic and social orders in effect began with the first shock of the French invasion—symbolized
by the dramatic confrontation of Napoleon's modern army
with the medieval Mamluk cavalry (armed with spears and
dressed in resplendent finery). The history of the Arab world
from Napoleon's invasion to the present may be viewed as
one of continuous struggle in one form or another against
Europe and its political, cultural, and economic domination.
Unlike Japan's, the Arab impulse to modernization was, at
least in its initial phases, exogenous: the inner need seems not
to have crystallized sufficiently to express clearly defined social
goals. When one reads al-Jabarti's[10] descriptions of the incuri-
ous reactions of Muslim scholars to the demonstrations by the
French of the wonders of European science, one is inclined to
think that, left to its own devices, late patriarchal society
would have had no interest in modernizing. (It seems that
only Japan, in the non-Western world—for specific social and
economic reasons—was able to respond to the West in an autonomous and selective way.)

In any event, the Arab subjects of the Ottoman Empire
could do nothing about the institutional (military, bureaucratic, legal) reforms imposed upon them, which ushered in
all subsequent change. By the second half of the nineteenth
century, there was no escape from the engulfing tide, which
had penetrated the traditional culture and created a new
Western-oriented elite. It would probably have been possible
to cope with the European onslaught even at that late stage,
had it not been for failure and collapse on the economic front.
Again here the contrast with Japan is illuminating. Whereas
Japan was fully aware of the consequences of foreign borrowing and so relied on domestic sources (mainly agricultural

surplus) to finance its industrialization process, the Ottoman Empire and Egypt borrowed from Europe without restraint, inaugurating the kind of foreign indebtedness and decapitalization which would continue into the twentieth century.

Neopatriarchal Responses to European Penetration

From the force of Europe's impact, a profound contradiction emerged between two cultural models: the rational, secular model, patterned after Western experience, and the traditional model, firmly based in the values of Islam.

It is in this tension between religious conservatism and Western secularism that the basic form of European political-cultural domination in modern times was reflected in Arab consciousness and experience. The essential development may be traced schematically: already by the early nineteenth century the Arab world had been largely incorporated into the European world system, and by the outbreak of the First World War it was a secure periphery of the capitalist world market. The relationship of dependency in economic and cultural terms was now firmly established. Neither the coming of political independence (following World War II) nor the establishment of Arab socialism (in the 1950s and 1960s) would overcome it or significantly loosen its grip. Within this relationship evolved, in the twentieth century, the *dependent* economy and state system of neopatriarchal society with its distorted political and economic structure. At the end of the century of neopatriarchy, political "independence" found expression not in Arab unity—the goal, since the Awakening, of three generations of Arab nationalists—but in a multiplicity of separate, antagonistic sovereignties, and the boundary of nearly every Arab state was drawn not by national will but by the European powers, in agreement among themselves. The internal structure of each state—the bureaucracy, courts, police, and army—was largely of Europe's making. Just as important was European and American influence on education and on culture generally: education from the kindergarten to the university level was patterned after Western models. Moreover, thought, literature, styles of living, and consumption were copied from Europe (and later America). Even where the West was unable to impose its will directly, as in some parts of the Arabian peninsula, its influence and its presence were soon fully felt.

All this occurred in the sphere of social practice. Internally, the development of political life revolved around two ideological movements, both stemming from the nineteenth-century Awakening: secular liberalism and Islamic reformism. Liberalism, with its emphasis on parliamentarianism, secular values, freedom of the press, and the market economy, expressed the interests of the rising urban middle class, spearheaded by the Christian professionals of Egypt and greater Syria. Closely linked to liberalism was the movement of Arab nationalism, which also found its earliest articulation in the writings of Syrian Christian intellectuals.

Islamic reformism, on the other hand, while not explicitly opposed to values of liberalism or nationalism as such, based itself on a view of a revived Islam, with religion rather than nationalism as its basic impulse and ground of unity. The contradiction between nationalism and militant (fundamentalist wing of) Islamic revivalism remained dormant, not coming to the fore until much later, when neopatriarchy reached a crisis point (which we will treat in Chapter 9).

After the First World War, national independence, limited and conditional, came to two major countries, Egypt and Iraq (the other two independent states in the interwar period were Saudi Arabia and Yemen). Both were established as monarchies based on parliamentary democracy and the doctrine of liberal nationalism. Surviving into the 1950s, these two regimes provided the concrete embodiment of the possibilities and limitations of Western-imported democracy. During the interwar period, Arab nationalism found expression in several political parties in the Fertile Crescent countries and, after the Second World War, was embodied in three principal movements, dominating political life until the end of the 1960s: the Movement of Arab Nationalists, the Socialist Baath party, and Nasserism. All three movements sought to replace the Western-type multi-party system and called for Arab unity and a form of socialism.

During this period, Islamic fundamentalism lagged behind, despite the relative success of the Muslim Brothers in Egypt; it would remain unable to break through to the surface of political life so long as liberal democracy and unitary, secular Arab nationalism were dominant and able to galvanize the political energy of society. But the collapse of Nasserism (after the defeat of the 1967 war), Baathism's failure to take up pan-Arab leadership (the split between Syria and Iraq), and the dissolution of the Movement of Arab Nationalists provided the opportunity for militant fundamentalism to assert itself.

The Modern Sultanate

The distance separating the moderate Islamic reformism of 'Abdu and Afghani from contemporary fundamentalism may be measured by the failures and setbacks of liberalism, nationalism, pan-Arabism, and the radical left over the preceding half century (1920 to 1970). Ironically, the end of politics in the Arab world (in the sense of political freedom expressed in a functioning multiparty system) came at the very moment when the great mass in most Arab countries had begun to acquire political consciousness and be integrated into the body politic—a result of universal elementary education, military conscription, the communications revolution, proletarianization, and urban expansion. So at the very moment that Arab patriarchal society appeared objectively ready for political change, it suffered a severe setback: instead of capitalist democracy or democratic socialism a political reversal occurred, a sliding-back to new forms of the petty sultanate based, as in the past, on unrestricted personal power, but rendered virtually impregnable (both in the "progressive" and conservative regimes) by the modern apparatus of control now available to the state.

The state, whether republican or monarchical, "progressive" or conservative (in ideology and social system), became embodied in a peculiar form of etatism: the state became the central controlling force in society, not just by virtue of its monopoly of coercion but also by its vastly increased economic power—as owner of the basic industries, source of all major investments, only international borrower, and provider of all essential services. In this form, the new sultanic state took upon itself much the same role of transforming society as had belonged to the European bourgeoisie in the early industrial age. But the power of the sultanate, unlike that of the bourgeoisie of the nineteenth century, grew at a much faster rate than the labor force and the economy. Commanding a vast budget derived from *sudden* accumulation of revenues (not only in the oil-producing countries), the state became within a few years the largest employer in society. And just as centralization of political power (which took place in all countries once national independence was secured) led to increasing authoritarianism, so sudden wealth brought with it increasing impoverishment (as a result of inflation and rising prices) and a dramatic widening of the gulf between rich and poor, leading, as we will presently see, to decisive shifts in the social structure.

But the rise of modern etatist sultanism, paralleled by the steady growth of Islamic fundamentalism, must be seen as the product of the same deep-rooted forces which produced the structure of neopatriarchal society—as the articulation of the traditional culture of patriarchy in the system of capitalist dependency brought about by Western imperialism.

6

Neopatriarchy in the Age of Imperialism

Direct and Indirect Domination

In what way did imperialism (understood as both colonialism and imperialism) contribute to shaping the sociocultural formation of neopatriarchy as we encounter it in the Arab world today? This question was partly dealt with in Chapter 5. We have seen how the first responses in the Ottoman Empire were basically defensive, reorganizing military and administrative institutions. These were the first, and in some respects the last, *autonomous* modernizing gestures against the European threat. Strictly speaking, all subsequent modernization unfolded within relations of *subordination* and *dependency;* under *direct* European domination, modernization became a function of the system of colonial rule and imperial domination. Thus to gain an adequate appreciation of the transformation patriarchal society underwent during the imperialist epoch, we need to understand the *objective* structures that emerged from the superimposition of European imperialism and colonialism upon patriarchal society.

First, we must make a clear distinction between the "colonized" and the "dependent" countries, to use the terms of Soviet social scientist Gleri Shirokov.[1] To the first group belonged Algeria, Libya, and Palestine, where French, Italian, and Zionist colonial policy aimed to settle the land and thus to dispossess the native inhabitants. To the second group, which enjoyed varying degrees of internal autonomy, belonged the rest of the Arab countries (except for Najd, Hejaz, and North Yemen). A parallel distinction (between direct and indirect domination) may be made in terms of the *socioeconomic* and *cultural* influences exerted by imperialism on the region as a whole.

The socioeconomic effects of each system are relatively easy to trace. In the countries under direct colonial rule the social structure was radically changed. In a relatively short time the population was dispossessed, uprooted, displaced, and reduced to total subordination to the colonial system. France and Italy resorted to old-fashioned colonial means, using force on a large scale to subdue the native populations. The Jewish Zionists, late comers to the colonial arena, used indirect methods at first (e.g., purchase of land), but later on, when Israel was established, resorted to the standard colonial tactics of force and forced dispossession. To the French, Italian, and Zionist settlers, the native population was just an obstacle to the colonial project, and in each case was treated as colonized peoples generally were, without much regard to human rights or international law.

The colonial system in its varied forms produced two types of native leaders, one nationalist and anticolonial, the other conservative and willing to cooperate with the colonial authorities. Both types belonged to the traditional society and drew their strength and status from its personalized relations of authority. In all three colonial regimes the principles of "divide and rule" governed the political approach to their colonies. The traditional leaders were often the instrument of this approach.

The effect of imperialist domination on the semi-independent countries was somewhat different, although the pattern of control and exploitation was essentially the same. For one thing, the expropriation of land, where it did occur (as in Tunisia and Morocco), remained limited, only tangentially affecting the existing social structure. Indeed, as noted earlier, the immediately felt effect of European domination was the total subordination of the economy to the interests of the metropolitan center. The consolidation of property claims of tribal and religious leaders and urban notables, in strengthening the traditional structure of authority (tribal, ethnic, religious), facilitated this subordination.

The upper crust of the native society was usually divided in its attitude toward the ruling power: opposition or collaboration were determined more by the possibilities offered for political accommodation with the colonial authorities than in terms of national demands. Strict differentiation in semi-dependent countries between quislings and nationalists within the leadership groups was not always as clear as it was in purely colonial settings. On the whole the traditional leadership tended to be more flexible and ready to reach some kind of understanding with the foreigner, spontaneously equating its own interests with the national interest (it always considered this interest better served by political accommodation than confrontational or revolutionary activity). The petit bourgeois and popular mass nationalists, on the other hand, tended to be much more firm in their demands for national *independence* and less ready to accept accommodation and compromise. Whence Shirokov's observation that in the "colonized" countries national opposition ended up as the movement of national *liberation,* whereas in the semi-independent countries it always took the form of a movement of national *independence.*[2]

Modernization of Patriarchy

The systems of colonialism and imperialism, in their "positive"—that is, cultural—impact, served to modernize patriarchal society and culture by producing new social and cultural forms and institutions which were modeled on Western experience and mediated through Westernized native elites.

The specific conditions under which this elite came into being, and the way it was educated, had great significance for its political development and ideological orientation. It was modernized partly by the new system of education and partly by direct contact with Europe and Europeans—through student missions, commercial links, travel, and so on. Modernization resulted from the acquisition of two kinds of knowledge: knowledge of a foreign language and knowledge of a European culture. For patriarchal society—or, initially, for its upper crust—this type of enlightenment was a transforming experience, quite unlike any other undergone by earlier encounters with Europe. At first, this French/English-educated secular generation now appeared to spearhead a genuine break with traditional culture and its stagnant ways. But it soon became evident that no real or quick break would be achieved. For, as mentioned earlier, modernization *within* the structure and relations of colonial or imperialist-dominated patriarchy was no more than a bastardized form of modernization: it only produced a "modernized" patriarchy.

The educated neopatriarchal elite quickly grew, in the post-independence era, from a small minority into a broad stratum of society, engulfing large numbers from the lower strata. Its proliferation, however, did not significantly alter its essential character. The values and attitudes of patriarchal relations internalized in early childhood underlay the "modernized" surface and determined the deep structure of personality and orientation.

The movement of Islamic radicalization accompanied the process of "modernization" and was dialectically linked to it. Islamic fundamentalism, like Westernization and "modernization," was a psychosocial phenomenon taking form under European domination and in direct reaction to it. But militant Islam (fundamentalism) ought to be interpreted not simply as a rejection of foreign values and ideas but rather as an attempt to give a new Islamic content to the meaning of self and society by reformulating a redemptive Islamic dogma. Thus it may be fairly said that in this instance a *radical* fundamentalist form of patriarchal reaction was to a substantial degree a product of European imperialism and modernization.

From the opposition, interaction, and confluence of these social and ideological currents, in the course of the last two or three generations, a distinctive intellectual elite emerged. It included traditional Muslim reformists and militant Islamic fundamentalists, as well as Westernized secularists, bound together, despite their ideological differences, by the same neopatriarchal intellectual structure and the same conscious and unconscious attitudes generated by Europe's political and cultural impact.

In its social stratification during the age of imperialism, "modernized" neopatriarchal society consisted of three distinctive strata: the impoverished masses; the petty bourgeoisie (inhabiting small towns and cities of the Arab world), and the ruling bourgeoisie, wielding all the power and nearly all the wealth. It was under the leadership, and in the shape of the ideas and goals, of this neopatriarchal bourgeoisie—the immediate and most finished social product of the imperialist age—that nominal national independence (dependency) and the contemporary state system of the Arab world were fashioned by the mid-twentieth century.

The Etatist Patriarchy

European imperialism may pride itself for having brought a variant of parliamentary democracy and bureaucratic government to many of the Arab countries. But its real legacy was rather different from these outward forms. Behind republic and monarchy, parliament and modern press, school and hospital, it provided the structures of the modern *etatist* state.

What made etatism so natural to neopatriarchal society is the fact that the former was essentially nothing but the medieval sultanate in modern form. For the distinctive characteristic of etatism, like that of the sultanate, is personalized (legal and extralegal) power, which finds expression in the coercive and suppressive apparatus of the state and derives its legitimacy not from some formal (constitutional or even traditional) source, but from the reality and possession of power. In this kind of polity the ordinary person is a passive entity, a subject not a citizen, with no human or civil rights or power to influence decisions concerning society as a whole.

In its structure etatism combined the paternalism of colonialism and the bureaucratic apparatus of the modern state. As such, it took upon itself all the functions of society. For individual citizens it was something external, poised over and against them. Free public association was impossible, even when guaranteed by the constitution, unless initiated and controlled by the state. Isolated, estranged, and suppressed, the individual subject was driven back to the primary social structures—the family, the ethnic community, the tribe, the religious sect—for security and for survival.

In this type of polity the gap between appearance and reality took on exaggerated forms. Here, for example, the most extreme idealism—whether political or religious—could co-exist, without conscious contradiction, with everyday cynical social practice. Stark contradictions between verbal and actual behavior produced no problematic tensions for consciousness. The individual may proclaim, on the level of ideas, total devotion to the social values of fatherland, unity, liberation, justice, equality, and so forth, and at the same time strictly adhere to private (family, ethnic, tribal) goals that have nothing to do with these values or may even contradict them. Etatism transplanted into patriarchal society not only eroded the positive values of traditional society, but also served to reify and alienate social relations.

As experience has shown, the etatist sultanate has an amazingly lasting power, far exceeding that of the traditional institution. Whether in the republican or the monarchical form, it has managed to persist in the face of all difficulties, including mass alienation, political dysfunction, economic chaos, attempted coups d'etat, and even military defeat.

cf al-Khald

Enlightenment, Exploitation, Terror

A western-trained Arab historian put forth the challenging thesis that before 1800 there was no such thing as an Arab *people,* Arab *society,* or Arab *world,* and that the Arab people, as a sociopolitical entity with a distinct self-conscious identity, is a recent growth—essentially the product of the nineteenth-century renaissance generated by Europe's direct political and cultural influence.[3]

To a certain extent, this thesis is true of all premodern, prenational formations. In the Arab context, it would make some sense if viewed from the standpoint of Europe's undisputed hegemony, beginning with 1798 (Napoleon's invasion of Egypt), and the social, political, and cultural consequences of its direct and indirect domination.

From this perspective, the Arab renaissance would no longer appear as an *autonomous* phenomenon, but rather as a special sort of development initiated and largely determined by the interaction between patriarchy and modernity under the conditions of domination. According to this view, it would seem as though the Arab world were *socialized* by Europe, that is to say, transformed from a disparate collection of isolated tribal, ethnic, and sectarian communities—strewn across the eastern and southern Mediterranean from Morocco to the Fertile Crescent, and loosely bound by the Ottoman Empire or subsisting in its shadow—into a "world" unified as a nation—at least on the level of culture and perception—with a common language, national consciousness, and perceived interests. From this standpoint the contemporary Arab world, as a social and political entity, is viewed as nothing more than a European creation.

If valid—and to a large extent it probably is—this view *why?* would necessarily imply a distorted and mutilated society, one plagued by (in Fanon's terms) the "mental sedimentation" and "emotional and intellectual handicaps" brought about by colonialism.[4] Fanon quotes the African intellectual Aimé

Césaire, who wrote about the "fear, inferiority complexes, trepidation, servility, despair, abasement" which European colonialism creates in the colonized—the obverse side of enlightenment.

So if enlightenment is the "positive" aspect of European imperialism, what is the character of an enlightenment grounded in "exploitation" and "terror?"[5]

These two aspects, one socioeconomic and the other psychocultural, combine to make European domination the ruthless destructive system that Fanon and Césaire wrote about. Once activated, this system of domination will blindly follow its logic to the end, until it succumbs to its internal contradictions or is disrupted by revolution and decolonization. Let us briefly survey some of the consequences of exploitation and terror created by imperialism-colonialism.

Exploitation in the colonized countries consisted of two movements: the expropriation of land and the dispossession of the colonized population. In the semi-independent countries exploitation was exercised indirectly, through "trade treaties, loans, friendly advice and pressure by ambassadors or gunboat diplomacy,[6] with the direct use of force being a last (though ever-present) resort. There was a basic difference in the way force was applied under the two modes of domination: in the colonies, the apparatus of coercion was present on the ground and could be used instantly and in any measure, while in the semi-independent countries, imperialism enjoyed only partial military presence (sometimes no direct presence at all) and could use force only intermittently, though no less ruthlessly and effectively (e.g., Egypt until 1952 and the Trucial Coast until the late 1960s).

The *range* of exploitation was determined by the objective limits of the individual situation. While in the semi-independent countries the given objective constraints delimited exploitation, in the fully colonized countries no clear limit was set, so that the range of exploitation depended solely on the colonizers' power—and sense of justice. In the prototypical colonies (Algeria, Libya, Palestine), the *mode* and *range* of exploitation were prescribed by the specific nature and goals of the individual colonial projects. But for all three the primary need involved appropriation and consumption of the totality of the country's natural and human resources.[7] Dependency theory, which provides some account of the economic and political conditions under which exploitation in the periphery took place, implies but does not fully expound the *terroristic* character of the process.

Terrorism, as a rational tool of domination and control, is a European invention and was initially applied to non-European peoples. Its success in the colonial world rested on one basic fact: overwhelming military superiority. Wherever Europeans and natives faced each other, terroristic practice was the colonizers' norm.[8]

It should be noted that neither the practice nor the theory which sanctioned and institutionalized it could have been sustained without the doctrine of European cultural and racial superiority—a doctrine implicitly or explicitly predicated on a view that placed Europe and the Europeans at the center of a world surrounded by backward, primitive cultures and peoples. After Hegel and the eighteenth-century philosophers, some of the strongest expressions of the spirit of European imperialism are to be seen in philosophical and "scientific" theories which put Europe at the center of world history, superior to the rest of humankind. Indeed, as Edward Said has forcefully shown,[9] the very *knowledge* Europe developed of non-European cultures and peoples, especially of "Eastern" or "Oriental" civilizations, was imbued with the predatory and racialist spirit of imperialism. Capitalist greed and colonial expansionism found their ready-made justifications in scientific theories, high moral aims, and the mission of civilizing the world.

On the ground and in actual practice, imperialism shielded itself against self-questioning and guilt mostly by displacing the violence it practiced onto its victims. As Fanon has shown, blaming the victim was a facile justification: as terrorists, the colonized became the legitimate object of almost any kind of violence undertaken against them. Rational terror would be applied legally and systematically over long periods of time without serious questioning in the center. In Algeria and Libya, and more recently in Palestine, homes would be routinely blown up, communities collectively punished, land arbitrarily confiscated, and men and women systematically jailed, humiliated, tortured, or displaced—a process generally labeled pacification. Colonial terror would traumatize successive generations, would dispossess and devastate them with its unbounded greed and violence.

The social and psychological consequences of this rational terror have not been fully analyzed. What, for example, have been its effects on the personality structure of the colonized? How has it influenced the common person's self-esteem? What impact has it had on the social structure—the extended family, the neighborhood, the close-knit traditional community? In what way and to what extent have learning and education in the shadow of colonial humiliation contributed to feelings of inadequacy vis-a-vis the European, to self-doubt and self-hate, to intellectual confusion and suppressed rage?

The "sediments" and the "emotional and intellectual" handicaps wrought by colonialist terror, perhaps not as visible as the symptoms of economic exploitation, may in the long run have been more destructive. Perhaps, then, any attempt to properly understand the all-pervasive crisis created by "modernization" in the epoch of imperialism must grasp the phenomena of colonial terror and exploitation and their social-psychological impact.

Can there be any doubt that the development of Arab society would have taken an altogether different form had the Arabs somehow succeeded, as did the Japanese, in modernizing while keeping Europe at bay, thus escaping the effects of the latter's predatory terror?

Imperialism, Islamism, and Islamic Fundamentalism

In one sense Islamism, as a movement of political emancipation and cultural revival, is the reverse side of Westernization; it is as much the product of the age of imperialism as are "enlightenment" and "modernization."

On the political-ideological level, the modern Middle East has seen three major responses to the social and political crisis created by the European onslaught. The first two, secularism and fundamentalism, represented, respectively, clear-cut acceptance of the European model and definite rejection of it. The third, which we call reformism, sought a middle ground. In each case, however, what we encounter is not a new ideology or social theory but rather forms of consciousness, within neopatriarchal society, that reflect varying responses to the problem of distorted modernization.

The only escape from direct domination by Europe lay in devising various forms of resistance; but even in areas where resistance seemed successful, the relations of dependency persisted and even grew stronger. The full significance of this fact becomes clear when we consider the Japanese case, the only historical instance of successful escape from direct European domination. The Japanese succeeded in warding it off precisely by virtue of their ability to embark on a course of *autonomous* modernization, enabling them to develop rapidly enough to prevent a military takeover of Japan. Of course, contributing factors were Japan's remoteness, insularity, and relative immunity to invasion (in contrast to the proximity, accessibility, and military vulnerability of the Arab world). But another, perhaps more important reason, is that at the point of breakthrough (Meiji Restoration in 1868), the Japanese patriarchal order, unlike the Arab (or Indian or Chinese), enjoyed two unique characteristics: political-territorial unity, and a *qualified* leadership.[10]

The first, and most pervasive and lasting, response of the

Arab patriarchal order, after being overwhelmed by Europe, was to take refuge in its religious tradition. Islam, as both an ideology and a model of social organization, became the natural rallying point of resistance, as exemplified in the four classic political-religious uprisings against imperialist domination—of Abdul Qadir against France in Algeria, of al-Mahdi against Britain in Sudan, of 'Umar al-Mukhtar against Italy in Libya, and of 'Izz al-Din al-Qassam against the British in Palestine. Significantly, throughout the colonial period resistance to European domination, the moment it touched the masses, was converted from a limited political movement initiated by the nationalist leadership into an Islamic mass uprising. During the period of struggle for independence, no *nationalist*-led uprising became a *mass* movement without Islam providing the ideological impulse to revolt.[11] Thus, the national and anticolonial struggle derived its inspiration and strength from the patriarchal tradition rather than the secular ideologies propounded by the educated elite (a fact which partly accounts for the lack of radical social transformation following the major national revolutions of the last half century).

The development of traditional or fundamentalist Islam into a militant political movement is difficult to understand without taking into account its dialectical relation to imperialism and modernization. Early fundamentalism drew its self-affirmation and its content as a militant movement from uncompromising opposition to European political and cultural domination. As a doctrine, it gained articulation not from some theoretical critique but in response to an intolerable sociopolitical situation. In retrospective vision it sought deliverance from the present by the restoration of the glorious Islamic past; and, basing itself on the rhetoric of the sacred texts, it proclaimed that an authentic Islamic society could be realized here and now, if only Muslims would return to the true path and unite in the struggle against the historic enemy of the faith. (We will analyze this phenomenon in its contemporary form in Chapter 9.)

Recall that tradition-oriented Islam, like most institutional religions, is essentially quietistic, conformist, ritualistic, and abstract. It is transformed into militant fundamentalism only by the action of new leaders or spokespersons responding to a situation of national crisis. The aggressive and absolutist character of fundamentalist ideology is thus not necessarily an essential feature of traditional doctrine; indeed, fundametalist fervor tends to abate and its power to disintegrate when peace and social equilibrium are restored.[12]

It is important to note that in the course of its struggle against imperialism, traditional Islam itself underwent a modernizing experience, not only in methods but to some extent in outlook and practice as well. It developed its own modes of political organization and accepted in a qualified way certain Western models of rationality and technique. Still, intolerant of difference and incapable of genuine compromise, it could only accept victory or martyrdom to bring struggle to an end. And once in power, it tended to become counterrevolutionary, and uncompromisingly bound to religious orthodoxy, moral purity, and political obedience.

The opposition between the fundamentalists and the secularists (nationalists and left radicals) was not over a religious or moral issue. It was essentially political. To the extent that secular nationalism was unable to deal successfully with the political problem of foreign domination, and unable to bring about Arab unity, they contributed to religious radicalism. The fundamentalist movement stood to benefit from the secularists' failure, just as from the success of imperialism.

Poised between conservative Islam and Arab nationalism, Islamic reformism sought to play a moderating role, politically and ideologically. It eventually failed in this effort, probably in part because it went too far on some issues and not far enough on others, but mainly because it tended to compromise on political questions and to address concrete issues in terms of abstract ideological principles. Its naive trust in "reason"—reformulated as *ijtihad*—engaged its proponents in theoretically interesting but politically futile debate. They advocated evolutionary change and called for liberal, parliamentary government based on enlightened Islamic principles. It is not surprising that they continued to form only a small minority whose influence, though somewhat significant in the formative phase of the Arab Awakening, was rather limited, and that they steadily lost influence during the succeeding phases of European domination, and during independence. Their ideas, unlike those of the fundamentalists, never found their way to mass audiences.

Thus we can form some idea of the extent to which the structure of imperialist domination had shaped political consciousness and practice in neopatriarchal society. To sum up, in the political domain imperialism was responsible for fragmenting the Arab world politically and economically, and for consolidating traditional patriarchal power (by "modernizing" it), thus for substantially contributing to the rise of neopatriarchy as we know it today. As a result, both socially and psychologically, and in terms of both class and ideology, neopatriarchalism's hold was able to become strong enough to sidetrack both meaningful political reform and genuine democratic development, and to prevent any form of Marxist or radical structure from taking root in society. Patriarchalism and imperialism must therefore be viewed as objective collaborators in hindering normal socio-political change in the Arab world. This unconscious alliance not only persisted into the period of national sovereignty (and dependency), but became even more effective as each of the newly independent Arab countries sought to consolidate its own sovereignty and independence. In the post-colonial Arab world, unity became almost as politically dangerous to the status quo as socialism— the latter being probably more feared there than it was in the capitalist Center itself.

European imperialism, then, may be said to have distorted social and political progress in two ways: by undermining normal economic development (capitalist growth)—particularly in Egypt, where since Muhammad Ali it effectively blocked industrial development and reduced the economy to agricultural production; and, at the same time, by obstructing the development of an urban working class, in that it preserved and strengthened the social and political structures of neopatriarchalism.

But the distorting impact of imperialism was perhaps most deeply felt in the cultural sphere. The colonization of consciousness (and the unconscious), seen in social and political terms, has perhaps influenced the development of the structure of neopatriarchy more than has military occupation or political domination. From this vantage point, the problem can no longer be regarded as conventional modernization theory sees it—as simply that modernization threatens "traditional society," or that the hardships of development rock an "underdeveloped" formation. Rather, the view must be taken that *patriarchal* society has been forced to appropriate European economic models and cultural paradigms under the distorting conditions of imperialist domination, cultural subordination, and economic dependency. Whence the lopsided character of "modernized" patriarchal (neopatriarchal) culture, with its pseudoscience, pseudoreligiosity, pseudopolitics, its political helplessness and cultural disorientation, and its distance from genuine modernity, that is, from authentic self-emancipation.

Cultural Hegemony

In a book published in Arabic in 1953, entitled *Missionary Activities and Imperialism in the Arab Countries,*[13] two Muslim intellectuals, one a medical doctor and the other an Islamic historian, launched a polemic against the Christian missions in the Arab world in the name of Arabism and Islam, attacking them as instruments of Western imperialism. They accused the missionaries of seeking to "corrupt the national character of the Arab and Islamic peoples"[14] by representing Arab Islamic culture as backward and by showing that "Western science and literature are superior."[15] The ultimate goal of missionary education, they maintained, was "to spread spiritual debility and to create feelings of inferiority that would lead to the Arab people's submission to Western imperialism."[16] What Khalidi and Farroukh tried to do, and came short of doing, was to uncover the nature of cultural imperialism. But they lacked the right perspective and the proper conceptual apparatus to do so, and their attack remained confined to what has become the familiar polemical-apologetic discourse of militant or fundamentalist Islam.

And cultural imperialism is not easy to grasp. Its illusive character derives partly from its pervasiveness and diffuseness—its power to mediate its effects in uses, habits, attitudes, and artifacts that escape immediate identification as instruments and mediations of domination. This characteristic of cultural imperialism reaches its highest expression in consumer society and the kind of consciousness it imprints on societies of the nonindustrial Third World. The "positive" aspects which accompany even the most repressive colonial regimes reside in the inevitable byproducts of enlightenment that come with the Western challenge. Viewed in Gramsci's terms, the *non-coercive coercion* of cultural imperialism may be seen as the broad process whereby the culture of the colonial rulers gets superimposed on the culture of the ruled.

Socially, the most obvious effect of this cultural dominance appears in the rise of a new class division (specifically in the oppositions of elite versus mass, urban versus rural), which parallels the one-sided dominance in the division between metropolitan center and peripheral society. This division provides a new dimension to the social hierarchy centered around the *effendi* class: the *khawaja*, the European counterpart of *effendi*, now makes his appearance as the parallel non-native symbol of status and power. The *khawaja* complex speaks for the inferiority of native culture and the superiority of everything European; thus "in order to be good, strong, able, and right" one has to be like the Europeans.[17] This reaction found its cognitive and objective embodiment in the adoption in most Arab countries of a new system of education, which the early missionaries played a major hand in establishing.

The Missionary Effect

The Christian missionaries were never fully trusted in the Arab world, not just on religious grounds, but also for political reasons. This suspicion is graphically brought out in Soraya Antonius's moving novel, *The Lord,* about Palestinian society under British rule. The principal of a missionary school in Jaffa puts it this way: "What are we teaching? What was the purpose behind our school? Were we really spies? And for whom? Or, much worse, were we going to convert the children and subvert the parents?"[18]

For their part, the missionaries, even the most humble and humane among them, regarded the natives in the same paternalistic way as the colonial administrators; but they also saw themselves as the teachers and guides who would dispel the darkness and ignorance weighing upon the native mind.

Howard Bliss, the second president of the Syrian Protestant College (later named the American University of Beirut), portrayed the "modern missionary" in an article published in the *Atlantic Monthly* in 1920.

> [He is] trained in the scientific method, he has risen from his studies in the broad aspects of Evolution, in Comparative Religion, in the History of the Philosophy of Religion, in the History of Civilization, in the Lower and Higher Criticisms [to represent] a superior Christian religion."[19]

To this person, while other religions were not invalid, Christianity was clearly superior. "Christianity is not Buddhism, it is not Mohammedanism [*sic*], however near these religions may come in some of their teachings to the teachings of Christ."[20] So the modern missionary, while perhaps not wishing to impose his or her religion on other believers, remains certain that the Christian view of the world is so superior to all other views as to make it "infinitely worthwhile to proclaim this view to the utmost parts of the earth."[21]

If the natives (both Muslims and eastern Christians) could not be converted, they would at least be given a true Christian education. The chief beneficiaries of this education were the children of the socially dominant Sunni Muslim and the well-off Christian families (in the Fertile Crescent and later in Egypt).

At the end of the First World War, Howard Bliss, called to testify before the peace conference at Versailles, had this to say about the Arab inhabitants of the former Ottoman provinces: They were a "long oppressed race" suffering from "timidity, love of flattery, indirectness. . . . They lack balance, they are easily discouraged, they lack political fairness, they do not easily recognize the limitations of their own right. They must therefore be approached with sympathy, firmness, and patience."[22]

Missionary education was, in certain essential aspects, modern and therefore radicalizing (just to teach a new language constituted a threat to the prevailing world-view); but it was also traditionalist and accommodationist. The missionaries discovered early on that in order to be able to teach they had not only to give up proselytism but also to harmonize the content of what they taught to existing belief and practice. This involved being on the side of the status quo in its political, ideological, and institutional aspects. Bayard Dodge, the first president of the American University of Beirut, expressed this attitude quite clearly in his inaugural address in 1923.

> We long to teach our students to regard the ideals of their parents with sympathy; to honor all who are charged with the official duties of their sects; to respect the motives of their ceremonies and rites; and to revere places of long-accustomed worship. . . . [W]e long to

make every student as loving, as pure, and as unselfish as Jesus was. The solutions of problems of race, hatred, and sectarian strife must be brotherly love. The way of attaining social decency and honest business is by pure conduct. The only answer to this world-wide question of poverty vs. wealth is unselfishness.[23]

At the same time, a clear ideological strain was transmitted with missionary education, grounded as it was in the values of individualism, pluralism, capitalism, humanism, and so forth, which portrayed the world and society in stable "natural" terms, "as something given"—to use Freire's words— "something to which man, as mere spectator, must adapt."[24] It is thus not surprising that the Arab enlightenment (the Awakening), most of whose early leaders were graduates of missionary schools, should from the beginning have been stamped by an idealistic, conformist orientation that stressed the didactic and adaptive rather than the radical or revolutionary approach to social change. This education produced an intelligentsia that from the very beginning sought to influence society more by "enlightenment and knowledge" than by revolutionary practice.

National Western-Style Education

Western-style education, at the same time that it made possible the emergence of a secular perspective, posited an opposite view, one respectful of Islam and tradition. In this sense, Islamic fundamentalism, as both ideology and militant political movement, may be construed as a product of cultural imperialism. Indigenous consciousness of the cultural tradition or heritage (*turath*), conceived as a mode of being or self-expression, is inconceivable without the contrasting secular and rationalist modes of seeing and knowing which Western education necessarily implied. Thus we see, in the literary and critical texts of the interwar period, and most clearly in Egypt, a line that divides the traditional writing from the new or contemporary writing. The interwar period as a divid-

ing line, not the *nahda* of the late nineteenth century, marks
the beginning of secularization in literature and politics. That
a genuine break actually failed to develop in the thought and
practice of the subsequent period of independence, and instead new forms combining patriarchal and modern features
ensued (neopatriarchy), need not diminish the abiding significance of the liberal interwar period for future intellectual
and political developments.

Let me return to the moment of jarring contrast between
traditional learning and Western knowledge (education) and
the riveting experience of wonder and discovery which the
transition from one to the other entailed. This experience is
graphically described in the memoirs of Taha Hussein, perhaps the leading liberal writer of the interwar period. One
day this poor blind student from al-Azhar finds himself for
the first time listening to a lecture at the Western-style Egyptian University by a Western-educated Egyptian professor.

> He [Taha Hussein] was amazed by something he had never before
> experienced at al-Azhar: the professor beginning his lecture with
> these words, "Gentlemen, I give you Islamic greetings, and say, may
> peace and God's mercy be upon you."
>
> At al-Azhar the youth was used to hearing quite another kind of
> address. There the sheikhs [on commencing a class] never addressed
> their students directly, but always turned to God, thanking Him
> and glorifying His name. Nor did the sheikhs ever greet their stu-
> dents, but sent prayers to the Prophet, his family and his com-
> panions.
>
> But what really shocked this youthful student was the shift to a new
> kind of authority, and a new way of expression.
>
> The youth was amazed when the professor did not begin with "The
> author, may God have mercy on him, said," but spoke on his own
> and without reference to any book. His words were perfectly clear
> and needed no explanation.[25]

When full political independence was achieved after the
end of the Second World War, cultural decolonization did
not accompany it. Indeed, with independence began an in-

direct—and, precisely because indirect, somewhat different but more pervasive—form of cultural colonization, whose hegemonic hold derived not from direct political or military control, but from the penetration of a new patriarchal elite by Western education, and from the domination of society by Western mass media and the values and wants of Western consumer society.

The institutions of higher learning which mushroomed throughout the Arab world in the postindependence period produced scientists but not science, medical doctors but not medical science, social scientists but not social science, and so forth. Their graduates were on the whole politically anti-Western, but they were culturally and psychologically profoundly Western-oriented, forming the most culturally dependent sector of society. This may be seen in the fact that as a group the Arab-educated elite of the post-World War II era tended to be reflexively resistant to Marxism. The West constituted the implicit matrix for measuring everything—from ways of dress to the proper education of children, to the correct path of economic development and "nation-building." Thus, for example, the natural form of social change, from the standpoint of this educated class, consisted in unquestioning adherence to Western principles of development. Change came about by control from the top and flowed from the top down; technocrats and highly trained individuals alone could effect modernization and change; revolution and violence only led to tyranny and chaos. It is not surprising that for this elite the most obvious obstacle to genuine change—dependence, lack of genuine autonomy—remained hidden or obscure. How else can the fact be explained that after over a century and a half of being open to the West the Arabs were still importing science and technology and unable to generate their own!

The difficulty in this ambiguity which is inherent in political liberation itself, is that political independence not only fails to end cultural dependency but provides new and more

favorable conditions for its expansion. It is in this context
that the notion of cultural revolution or cultural break ac-
quires its meaning, pointing to a struggle more difficult than
the political and less quickly won.

The Educational Foundations

In the postindependence age, the educational and philan-
thropic foundations played much the same role as the missionaries had in the preindependence era; and like the early
missionaries, most of these foundations were American.[26]
The foundations aimed beyond the missionaries' goals;
they were interested not only in education but also in extra-
academic research, in development programs, in technical
training, in activities that had far-reaching political and ideological implications. The fact that after World War II the
majority of the educated men and women were graduates of
American colleges and universities greatly facilitated work
of the foundations, whose efforts now focused on American
institutions in the region, emphasizing social science research
and development and planning programs.

It is hard to measure the influence the foundations had on
the shaping of the postindependence (English-speaking) intelligentsia of the Arab world, but it is clear that they substantially strengthened Western educational structures and the
use of English as the language of scientific communication, as
well as the privileged place assigned to empirical social science and American modes of thinking and doing.

American foundations in the Arab world (and in Third
World countries generally) have not been as selflessly philan-
thropic or disinterested as they are presented to be; many of
their activities were closely linked to the political, ideological,
and economic interests of the United States.[27] Foundation
money has played an important role in deflecting energies and
resources in certain areas and directions, resulting in a bene-
ficial effect from the standpoint of the status quo and of

United States policy. By stressing pragmatism and the evolutionary approach, the foundations here helped to discourage more radical views and methodologies, and by encouraging some of the most talented intellectuals to become engaged in micro-research and modernization, they have prevented possible revolutionary changes from occurring.[28] The model of training that was put forth aimed at producing leaders who were intellectually and ideologically attracted to the "perspectives and the political and economic institutions of the United States."[29]

7

The Neopatriarchal Discourse

Woard fushr Lord!
with collision

Language and Discourse

Language, as Barthes has described it, is simultaneously a social institution and a system of values.[1] In its narrow sense discourse is a form of language: larger than a sentence but smaller than a total language.[2] The term discourse, as I use it here, includes this denotation but goes beyond it to assimilate the objective realities of language emphasized in Barthes' definition. As in Frederic Jameson's precise terms, these objective realities refer to " 'realities' or objects in the real world, such as the various levels or instances of a social formation: political power, social class, institutions, and events themselves."[3]

The "language" of the neopatriarchal discourse is classical Arabic, in which the knowledge (beliefs, concepts, substantive information) and self-knowledge (modes of self-understanding and of self-relating) of neopatriarchal culture get formulated and produced in the shape of discourse. One of the most striking characteristics of what we call classical Arabic (*fusha*) is the radical dichotomy it presupposes between the everyday colloquial and formal language: the division is not merely that between literate and vulgar tongues found in all class societies, but between two distinct *languages,* structurally related but essentially different. One spontaneously absorbs one of these from one's environment in the process of growing up, then has to appropriate the other as *another* language, much as a foreign language. The difference between colloquial and classical Arabic involves something close to the difference existing between, say, modern French and medieval Latin. There is no other society in the world today that uses its traditional classical language practically unchanged as its basic means of bureaucratic communication and formal discourse.[4]

A major implication of this rift has been the reinforcement of traditional social divisions and the concealment of the modern material and class basis of cultural disparity: knowledge becomes a privileged possession, an instrument of power. Linguistic competence (familiarity with classical literature and the ability to use the classical language forcefully in public speaking) bestows status and power, and by the same token the illiterate and semi-literate are excluded from this power. Their consciousness is formed largely outside the culture of the public educational institutions and the media (which are geared by their language to literate audiences). Theirs is a folk knowledge and a folk culture.

In the process of socialization, the classical language plays an even more fundamental role in shaping orientation and attitude: it determines the form and content of the child-rearing and educational practices of society at large. Normally the child's first encounter with the classical or literary language is through the sacred text, which children are often made to learn by heart. From the very beginning the child thus experiences a dissociation between *learning* and *understanding*. One's early spontaneous attempts at questioning and clarification (i.e., meaning, understanding) are aborted, and rote learning, based on memorization and the rejection of all questioning, becomes the normal way of acquiring ideas and internalizing values.[5] The mode of thought deriving from this sort of training, reinforced in the subsequent stages of socialization, is characterized by a peculiar capacity to resist external challenges either by rejecting them altogether or by absorbing them into the self, but without experiencing change. Thus, as we shall see later, the European model of rational inquiry appropriated by the thought of the Awakening becomes largely a fetishized norm manipulated, in support of its own particular "rationality," by the reformist, the secularist, the nationalist, and the fundamentalist.

Reading and Interpretation

If language structures thought, classical Arabic structures it in a decisive way. This is not only because of the essentially ideological character of this language with its rigid religious and patriarchal framework, but also because of its inherent tendency to "think itself," that is to say, to impose its own patterns and structures on all linguistic production. It is a "received language," "a language of others," and it favors, as Halim Barakat puts it, "literary over scientific writing and rhetoric over the written text and speech over writing."[6]

Classical Arabic produces a sort of discourse that mediates reality through a double ideology: the ideology inherent in the "trance of language"[7]—produced and reproduced by the magic of catchwords, incantations, verbal stereotypes and internal referents—and the ideology supplied by the "encratic"[8] language—produced and disseminated under the protection of political or religious orthodoxy. This sort of discourse is especially suited for the projection of a particular kind of being, for organizing the irrational, and for activating the "social imaginary" (Castoriadis).

As Jacques Berque rightly points out, such discourse can provide all the terminology of modernity, but its connotations do not necessarily refer to modernity as lived experience. In Berque's words, "Who would claim that its connotations refer to . . modernity? Does its true 'referent' not lie elsewhere?"[9] For its field is the rhetorical rather than the scientific, the metaphysical rather than the metonymic: "Its fatherland is the general."[10]

The priority given speech over writing, as noted by Barakat and Adonis, has far-reaching implications, to which I can here only briefly allude. This tendency should be assessed in itself, as an independent factor lying outside all considerations of literacy or education. In Europe, for example, the invention of printing, among its major effects, made the Bible available on a wide scale, thus serving to spread and deepen the Protestant revolution. The individual act of *reading* the Bible constituted an intellectually revolutionary development in that it brought about a crucial transition, which might be described as a transition from rhetoric to hermeneutics. In the Arab world traditional patriarchal culture never promoted the *reading* of the Quran, even after it became widely available following the introduction of printing in the nineteenth century. To this day it is still recited, chanted, and repeated by heart but not, or rarely, *read*. *Interpretation* has remained the monopoly of specialists or religious officials, whose exegesis, moreover, derives less from the sacred text than traditional commentaries on it.

In this context attention should be drawn to the subversive and liberating function of reading, and the primary concern of all established orthodoxy to protect itself against all *critical* reading or interpretation, that is, understanding. Subversion or liberation is attained by this sequence: reading (interpretation), understanding, criticism. So if reading is the path to innovation and change, speech—monopolized by orthodoxy and the status quo—is the condition of stability and continuity. Hence the centrality of the *monologue* in all forms of neopatriarchal discourse—in the modes of expression and interpersonal interaction and in terms of the values and relations that validate and reinforce them.

The monological mode of discourse manifests itself, for instance, in the tendency of speakers persistently to exclude or ignore other speakers. But this mode also appears in the very structure of the discourse itself: not just authority produces the monological discourse, but also the language itself, in that it privileges rhetoric and discourages dialogue.

Neopatriarchal discourse, in addition to its social and psychological implications, has important epistemological consequences of which the most important perhaps is the way in which truth or validity is constituted. All monologues, in insisting on agreement, exclude difference, questioning, and qualification. Hence monological speech (and writing) typically never exhibits hesitation or doubt—attributes that delimit or undermine monological authority—but relies on general and unqualified affirmation. The fundamental type of monological truth is absolute truth and its ultimate ground revelation. Clearly, the monological discourse is, by its very structure, a negation of dialogue and of the assumptions on which it is based: the assumption, for example, that no discourse is in itself final or closed, that only free questioning can yield true knowledge, or that truth is constituted not by authority but by discussion, exchange, and criticism.

The monological discourse may be expressed in different forms and articulated in different voices, depending on its setting. Thus in the household the father's is the dominant discourse, in the classroom the teacher's, in the religious gathering or tribe the sheikh's, in the religious organization the *'alim's,* in the society at large, the ruler's, and so forth. This discourse derives its perceived sense of signification from the structure of language itself rather than from the individual utterance. While the structure reinforces authority, hierarchy, and the relations of dependency, it also produces oppositional forms typical of the neopatriarchal discourse: gossip, backbiting, storytelling, and silence. For discussion or opposition in these settings can only be carried out behind the back of authority, or underground, never face to face in open exchange.

Monological speech, in daily practice, rarely produces good listeners, for it aims not to enlighten but to dominate. The listener-recipient, the *other* of the monological relationship (the son, the student, the subject), is reduced to silence: one may outwardly acquiesce, but inwardly one turns away. Hence the ambiguous relation of the illiterate masses to authority, orthodoxy, and high culture. Colloquial or oral culture is in this respect like the culture of children or the counterculture of rebels—both of whom turn away, withdraw, and remain silent without engaging in overt or direct opposition.

It is not difficult to see why in the monological culture silence tends to reign; apart from the effect of censorship and intimidation, the social majority—that is, the poor, the young, and women—is permanently reduced to the status of listeners ("they listen [to] the word," i.e., obey). This majority's world is inhabited by multiple single voices that command and legislate its life from above.

If in a monological culture validation rests (as it does in neopatriarchal society) on the spoken word ("so and so said *ḥadīth* that so and so said that so and so said"), then nonverbal proof (empirical evidence) is rendered secondary or even irrelevant. Thus the world of objects and events tends to be reduced to authoritative verbal representations that possess their own system of validation. So the anecdote becomes the document and the evidence: to narrate is to reveal and to make intelligible.[11] Praxis becomes a function of narrative: the telling of the action is the action itself.[12] Indeed, events acquire their significance only in the telling. The ontological differentiation between the action and its verbal formulation is so blurred that its terms intermingle and often lose their separate identity.

In this kind of discourse the ideological component is to be sought not merely in the explicit content but also in the presuppositions implicit in its linguistic structure. This aspect becomes clear when we recall the ideological specificity of classical Arabic we alluded to earlier. Thus ideology presents itself on two levels, the manifest level of the text, taken as a whole, and the underlying level of the linguistic categories. We can easily grasp the first level, the ideological power function of the text in its institutional and formal expressions, and these explain why in the neopatriarchal discourse ideological thinking is so far ahead of the critical. The effect of the unconscious and implicit categories, however, is more difficult to pin down. Roman Jakobson's characterization of speech-systems is of special relevance here: a speech-system should be defined less by what it permits us to say than by what it compels us to say.[13]

One way of dealing with this aspect of the monological discourse is to analyze its cultural context, that is, to look at changes in meaning that result from changes in linguistic context—for example, the process of coding and recoding which takes place in the translation of one mode of expression into another or of one "language" into another. In translations from a *foreign* language the richness of classical Arabic makes it seem easy to overcome the problem of translating terminology and recoding. But this appearance does not take into account the shift in context and the way categories and terms are grounded in specific meanings and experiences. Nor is this difficulty in translating or understanding overcome merely by adequation of language—that is to say, by gaining linguistic competence in the foreign language without however achieving an inner grasp of its cultural context, that is, the unified structure of concepts, categories, and linguistic codes.

Failure to resolve this difficulty, and total unawareness of this failure, is evident in the (unconscious) recoding which occurs in the Arabic translation of Western texts (both linguistic and cognitive). They are transformed in the process of being recast in new (Arabic) linguistic forms. An extreme but illuminating literary example is Mustafa al-Manfaluti's popular novel, *al-Fadilah* (*Virtue*), the translation or Arabic rendering of *Paul et Virginie*.[14] Here the transposition of character, plot, meaning, and motivation into the context of the classical Arabic and Egyptian culture is so complete as to render the original work virtually unrecognizable—an exemplary neopatriarchal literary product. Here as elsewhere adaptation is the mechanism whereby the process of shifting from one context to another is carried out, a process of *ta'rib* (literally, Arabization), through which the original text is *transformed* into Arabic.

This failure to penetrate the alien cultural text from the "inside," and to appropriate it comprehensively as a translated meaning or content, sheds some light on another phenomenon involving a movement of interpretation between different contexts or cultural backgrounds: the parallel failure to transfer scientific and technological knowledge, despite exposure to European science as early as the first student missions to Paris in the 1820s. Student missions are still sent out to acquire basic scientific knowledge in the West, a century and a half later.[15]

On the other hand, one of neopatriarchy's most notable successes has been the evolving of an effective defense against the charge of failure: an apologetic doctrine based on a vision of the Arab past which (in this vision's more vulgar forms) reduces Western civilization to a product of Arab or Islamic civilization. The success of this maneuver in turn points up the central shortcoming of the Arab Awakening: its failure to confront Europe on its own terms (as did the Japanese), to recognize the terms of modernity, and to attempt an epistemological or paradigmatic *break* with its patriarchal past.[16] In this light even the linguistic or "language" problem no longer appears as the serious one of adequately transposing meaning from one culture to another, but reverts to one of a structural dysfunction occurring within the framework of the awakening consciousness itself. Thus neopatriarchy, while consenting to the modernization of its material life by accepting the concepts of "science" and "progress," sought immediately to repress the radical questioning which briefly appeared at the beginning of the Awakening.

From the very outset, the traditional (patriarchal) discourse, with its closed reading of history and society, was never seriously challenged: on the contrary, it was preserved intact and placed alongside the emerging "scientific" or "modern" discourse. This fateful compromise meant there could be no possible divergence from orthodox ideology: from the start, the new (neopatriarchal) culture necessarily took an affirmative

rather than critical form in its discourse, as it was developed
by the rising literati in the three centers of neopatriarchal intellectual life for the next three generations (1880–1950)—
Beirut, Cairo, and Damascus.

In concluding this section I must underscore a point which
our earlier discussion did not stress, namely, that the impossibility of making the epistemological break was probably a
foregone conclusion under the conditions of the Arab Awakening—that is, the conditions created by the extension of European hegemony by the early nineteenth century. Within
this crucible the neopatriarchal discourse was born, and it
was reproduced in the context of Arab dependency and Euro-
American domination.

The Different Languages of Neopatriarchy

If we were to map out in a schematic way the development of
the neopatriarchal discourse from its early stages in the late
nineteenth century—from the suppression of questioning and
sceptical impulses, and their replacement by an affirmative
paradigm—to its final stage in the 1970s and 1980s, we would
be able to trace the following ideological pattern:

Ideological Phases of the Neopatriarchal Age

Orientation 1880–1918	Doctrine 1918–1945	Political Practice	
		1945–1970	1970–Present
Reformist (Islamic) "Progress," "reform"	Salafiyyah Islamic revival	Socialism Revolutionary wave	Fundamentalism
Secularism "Democracy"	Nationalism Unity	Modern sultanate Multistate system	Secular criticism

Again it is important to note that the neopatriarchal paradigm which developed over the last hundred years was the
product not simply of a philosophical failure, but rather of

social and historical realities which we should elaborate further.

In its early phase the development of the reformist and secular paradigm must be seen against a backdrop characterized by the development of trade, the expansion of cities and towns (for the first time since their decline in the thirteenth and fourteenth centuries), and the rise of a commercial and comprador bourgeoisie—a period ending with the First World War. During this phase the *mass* of society was out of the social picture. The movement into the cities only began after World War I, and the political and social integration of the proletarian and semiproletarian majority did not take place until after 1945, and in some countries much later.

In the last hundred years, the neopatriarchal discourse may be said to have developed in three "languages," each with its own vocabulary and concepts, grounded in a world and a subculture, different yet connected to the others. The first, the world/culture of the peasant and the tribal countryside, is divided from the other two not only by social and economic differences but also in psychology and outlook—the linguistic difference between classical and colloquial, the mental difference between literate and illiterate, and so on. The other two worlds are urban. Within the city are two different worlds/cultures: that of the urban proletariat and lower petty bourgeoisie, which forms an extension of the countryside; and that of the middle and upper bourgeoisie, the world of economic well-being, and high culture. It should be noted that these three worlds/cultures are neither self-sufficient nor self-enclosed, and although their constitution is largely based on class division they cannot be accounted for solely by means of the category of class. Social circulation, particularly in the last two or three decades, has blurred the division between rural proletariat, urban proletariat, and urban petty bourgeoisie, but at the same time the gap, separating all three from the urban upper-class formed by wealth and power, has widened.

Phases of Neopatriarchal Development, 1880–1980

Ottoman phase 1880–1918	Reformism and secularism; Islamic reform, science, democracy
European phase 1918–1945	Nationalism, Islamism, socialism, liberation, Arab unity; Islamic revival; socialist theory
Independence phase 1945–1980	Multistate system, capitalist and noncapitalist development; nationalism, socialism, Islam
Postindependence 1980–Present	Islamic radicalism, secular criticism; militant fundamentalism, liberal and socialist secularism

Recall that the language of the countryside, the colloquial dialect of the predominantly illiterate tribal, peasant, and village population, is still (in the late 1980s) that of over three-quarters of neopatriarchal society's members; that the rural discourse, enclosed in the local vernacular, is the product of the oral culture of the countryside—the beliefs, legends, and traditional practices of village and desert life. It is thus the most traditional (patriarchal) discourse of neopatriarchal society, for in the oral culture of the rural world the horizons of the spoken language and the traditional values and beliefs may be said to coincide in frozen symmetry. Indeed, the silence and passivity of the rural workers (tenants, sharecroppers, proletarians, independent subsistence farmers), the backbone of neopatriarchal society, is grounded in their illiteracy. Here the problem of illiteracy/literacy is not simply a question of reading and writing. Seen in the context of the literate language (classical Arabic)—of the division between a written and an oral culture—illiteracy constitutes a linguistic as well as a psychological disability probably without parallel in other Third World countries. For people to make the transition into literacy, they must not only learn a system of signs, but must also internalize a system of values which has no relevance to the daily existence of the rural population. In the literacy campaigns, the process of learning the written (classical) language becomes a kind of ritual in which the profane (the everyday) has to be suppressed and subordinated to the sacred text. Instead of intellectual windows being opened for the newly literate, the latter are brought closer to authority and its controls. Functional illiterates, the invariable product of all anti-illiteracy campaigns—men and women who can perhaps sign their names and read the headlines of a newspaper and make out the drift of a newscast—are still unable to *read.*

The classical language, by its very character, produces or reinvents the same mental obstacle that the attempts at overcoming illiteracy presumably seek to remove: dependency. Even as literacy spreads, *illiteracy* is preserved and compounded, for the power of the language is such that it inhibits the appropriation of any kind of alternative paradigm; literacy only reinforces the power of the monological discourse. For the rural workers, breaking the vicious circle occurs by other, unintended social means—being conscripted into the army, immigrating to the city, gaining regular access to urban culture through improved communications, and so forth—developments which over the last two or three decades have been responsible for the spontaneous breakdown of the isolation of rural life, though not for bridging the social and psychological gap separating city from countryside.

The Traditional Discourse

The literate language of the neopatriarchal city naturally divides into two kinds of discourse, one expressed in the traditionalist (patriarchal) language of the sacred texts, the other in the language of the progressive (reformist or secular) ideologist, the neopatriarchal language of the daily newspaper. Though the two discourses and their linguistic modes may differ in form as well as content, they are not essentially antagonistic, for in both their agreements and their oppositions they share the same basic paradigm.

Let us first address the traditional (Islamic) discourse. The power of this type of discourse, and the language through which it is expressed, derives from an authoritative origin or text, on which it bases its claim to truth and validity. This claim serves to achieve two things simultaneously: to consolidate the hegemony of the text (source) and to block the possibility of its criticism or replacement (i.e., the expression of what has not already been expressed in or through it). Here not only are certain domains of thought automatically sealed off, but the method of thinking itself is disarmed by rigid restriction to traditional modes—commentary, exegesis, recitation, and so forth. Thus the role of language in the traditional discourse, both in its theoretic and social use, is not so much to communicate or clarify as to impose obedience. In other words, the aim of the traditional discourse is to bring about not awareness, understanding, self-consciousness but its opposite—to reinforce an affective, noncritical state rooted in external dependence and inner submission. Whence the necessity of a system of knowledge based on rote learning (including learning the modern academic text) and the cultivation of intellectual passivity and uncritical submission to the printed page. Thus, to borrow a familiar phrase, here the text is everything and nothing exists beyond it; not because of a linguistic theory, but as a result of a metaphysical assumption: the traditional discourse, whatever form its expression takes, excludes every other discourse, for it not only contains the only true knowledge but the solution to all problems theoretical or practical. The only problematic this position concerns itself with is the social reinstatement of "true" Islam, the sole condition for the salvation of the individual and society.

The cognitive system in which the traditional discourse is grounded is designed to assure the supremacy of the religious perspective and automatically to delegitimate different or opposing positions. To accomplish this, a mode of presentation is stressed for which only a certain kind of knowledge is possible and in which all other types are excluded. Certain forms of cognitive dissonance and corresponding forms of (social) ignorance are cultivated, partly by direct ideological censorship, partly by reducing all questioning to the self-evident, and partly by making social reality appear "natural." This system of knowledge develops its own logic and ways of interpretation which are often impervious to evidence and persuasion and which function only in accordance with their own absolute categories. (One wonders, for example, what would happen if the sacred text were translated into the common tongue and its cognitive categories, so that it became immediately intelligible as did the Bible at the beginning of the European modern age.)

It is important to note, however, that this inflexible opposition to doubt, questioning, and change (toward modernity) derives not only from doctrinal or ideological considerations but mainly from practical, political concerns. Indeed, the traditionalist Islamic discourse in its various forms (reformist, conservative, fundamentalist) is concerned as much, if not more, with political power as with religious purity. We will have occasion later to deal with this central theme.

The Reformist or Secular Ideological Discourse

Alongside the traditional text stands the "newspaper" text of the reformist or secular ideological discourse of the bourgeois-petty bourgeois cultural sector. In this discourse the classical language is no longer tied to the sacred texts but is "modernized," that is, streamlined to fit the requirements of the times. Still, this new version of classical Arabic is in structure and tone essentially the same as the classical language of medieval Islam. Its "modernization" is a superficial, nonstructural change which took place under the influence of the literary revival of the late nineteenth century and the sudden exposure to Western knowledge. "Modern" classical Arabic evolved into "newspaper" Arabic—an easier, suppler language than

the traditional classical—in which the new literature and learning as well as the new popular media found expression. This
language coexisted harmoniously and without contradiction
with the traditional discourse, but not with the colloquial or
oral discourse of the common masses, as we shall see presently.
The claim that the "newspaper" Arabic of neopatriarchal society constitutes a synthesis between the colloquial and the
classical, as does, for example, modern French between medieval Latin and the spoken language, is an exaggeration, more
wishful thinking than reality. This simplified classical Arabic,
like the social formation it reflects, is neither fully traditional
nor really modern; it is an uneven combination of the two.
There existed no conscious or self-directing control over the
forces and developments which produced this language, with
the result that the essential division or opposition between
the colloquial and the classical (in both its traditional and
"newspaper" forms) remained unchanged. This fact has been
instrumental in preserving the social and cultural divisions
of neopatriarchal society, in maintaining the epistemological
compromise of the Arab Awakening, and in blocking the possibility of a genuine break with the patriarchal discourse.
Clearly, under these conditions, no breakthrough toward full
modernity was possible.

This problem appears throughout the three phases mark-
ing the cultural and political formation of neopatriarchal society in the last hundred years: the late Ottoman phase (to
the end of World War I), the period of European domination
(to the end of World War II), and the age of independence
(post-World War II to the present). Thus, the Ottoman phase,
which saw the rise of the first class of intellectuals who tended
to identify with the emerging urban bourgeoisie, brought into
use the new vocabulary, culled from the great Arabic classics,
and laced with the concepts and terminology of European
thought.[17] The newly discovered Arabic classics, now printed
for the first time in Beirut and Cairo as well as in Europe,
projected the image of the "glorious Arab past," obscured un-

til the Awakening by Ottoman oppression and cultural backwardness. For Muslim reformists as well as secular intellectuals living in the late Ottoman empire, the revival of society and the restoration of the Arab cultural and national identity implied, above all, breaking away from Ottoman political and cultural domination.[18]

But the cultural problematic, unlike the political, received, as we have seen, no clear-cut resolution: the issues implicit in the process of cultural revival, being not as simple, were neither clearly formulated nor fully confronted. The sacred and literary texts were inscribed in the new discourse of the Awakening without any critical awareness and set up as the finished models of reformist and secularist consciousness. The four hundred years of "decline" were seen as an aberration or an accident, so that the movement toward change was to be directed more to correct or purify society than critically to determine the content and goal of change. Thus the need to interrogate the past and to reassess its values from a critical standpoint did not arise or, if it did, was swept aside as unnecessary. It is therefore not surprising if the classical (traditional) paradigms were merely refurbished and "modernized" rather than reformulated or replaced, and were adopted enthusiastically by the educated strata, who were interested in any case not in questioning tradition or established authority but in reforming society to "catch up with the caravan of progress and civilization."

The next period, that of European domination, saw the expansion of the secular and liberal bourgeois intelligentsia. Now, following the end of the First World War, Europe became politically and culturally a direct, pervasive presence in the Arab world. The system of education was rapidly Europeanized and an increasing number of students traveled to study in Europe. Despite its more modern education, though, this interwar generation of intellectuals did not go beyond the epistemological boundaries set by the previous one; it exhibited the same docility toward the established order and its world-view. Thus the two dominant ideological currents of this period, Islamic reformism and liberal secularism, were the ones that had dominated the previous (Ottoman) phase, with only one difference: an enhancement of the secular liberal current, reflecting Europe's dominance and the spread of European-style education.

The period of independence, the era of ideological struggle and the multistate system, witnessed the eclipse of the reformist, liberal, nationalist, and socialist modes of discourse and the rise of Islamic fundamentalism, first as a defensive reaction, then increasingly as an aggressive alternative discourse.

In sum, the discourse of neopatriarchal society during the last century or so never, in any of its forms, took on a genuine or consistent critical position in addressing the social, political, or ideological issues of this age of transition. Its political thought remained essentially abstract and utopian, serving more to reinforce the established order than to question the latter's political and ideological foundations; and it remained totally inhibited in the face of the traditional religious discourse.[19]

An important social development during the independence period was the structural transformation of the educated social strata, resulting from the spread of education and the rise to social dominance of the petty bourgeoisie. It should be recalled that terms for education and culture are synonymous in Arabic, and the title "educated" (*muthaqqaf*, intellectual) is attributed to practically anyone who has achieved a college degree or a certain amount of formal education. A definite or clear class correlation of intellectuals was no longer possible; education and being educated now embraced individuals from all classes, including to some extent the proletarian masses. Membership in the "educated" (i.e., intellectual) class was no longer confined, as it had been before the 1950s, to an elite composed of a relatively small group of writers, teachers, artists, professionals, and other individuals; such membership now meant being part of a large, continually growing body of

a vocal group dominated by the petty bourgeois class. The intelligentsia in the classical age of Islam—the poets, the *ulema*
(sing., *'alim,* learned in religious matters), the scholars—was
largely dependent on the sultan's largess for its well-being.
Now in the age of independence, a similar situation obtained:
the intelligentsia was again the servant of the state; from its
ranks came the state ideologues as well as the subservient top
civil servants and technocrats.

The three phases in which the neopatriarchal discourse developed in its various forms may be characterized by the mode
of conceptualization distinctive of each phase. For example,
in the Ottoman period, during which the dominant mode of
neopatriarchal thought was shaped, the view of science was
fundamentally ideological, with little if any grasp of scientific
theory and method. The Awakening's *ideology* was based on
scientism while its *epistemology* remained bound to patriarchalism. This duality was expressed in the slogan, now revived
by fundamentalism, Science and Faith (*al-'Ilm w'al-Iman*), the
ground of simultaneously assuring ideological purity and social power. Unlike Japan, which at that very moment was systematically importing European science and technology and
converting them into effective conceptual and instrumental
possessions, Arab neopatriarchy was cultivating a literary-reli-
gious attitude toward Europe, history, and self-identity. From
the start it robbed itself of the opportunity to develop—as the
Japanese did with amazing consistency—an autonomous, self-
directing position which would, as it absorbed the shock of
Europe, pave the way to scientific understanding. A curious,
persistent blindness seemed to prevent this early generation
(but also the following ones) from grasping the fundamental
opposition at the heart of Western thought between science
and ideology, the implications of which the Japanese seemed
to have clearly understood from the very beginning. As a result, the Arab consciousness remained curiously passive or ar-
rested, poised at a pre-scientific, literary-ideological level, productive of only *naive* thought.

Nor was the mode of conceptualization during the following period (of European domination) radically different. The basic difference is that the generation of this period learned to speak a European language, English or French, through the modernized educational system. Thus a *fourth* language made its appearance alongside the other three—the colloquial, the traditional classical, and the "newspaper" classical—as a medium of expression and communication.[20]

Perhaps the single greatest failure of this first foreign language-speaking generation of intellectuals was its inability to bridge the epistemological gap inherited from the previous generation (which the Japanese had by now, 1920–1945, long since transcended). These intermediate intellectuals remained torn between tradition and modernity, between naive thought and scientific thought, and between the worlds posited by this opposition. The causes of this failure are not hard to point out. On the level of comprehension, the conflict manifests itself in the shortcomings of their new intellectual possession, their linguistic grasp. While bilingual intellectuals of this generation could speak, read, and write a foreign language, most of them lacked a real grasp of its idiomatic or paradigmatic structure. An English or French speaker, for example, might speak the language fairly fluently, but his/her discourse would still be a "naive" discourse, almost a word-for-word rendering comprehensible only by reference to the paradigms of the written (traditional or "modern") classical language. Translation into the Arabic illustrates the paradigmatic imprisonment of the naive and pre-scientific or literary thought of these neopatriarchal intellectuals. Though some of them— for example, Taha Hussein, Tawfiq al-Hakim, 'Abbas al-'Aqad, and some of the younger generation of European and American-trained intellectuals and writers of the 1930s and 1940s—wrote and spoke with a new voice, particularly in the fields of literature and history, their ideas and techniques were based largely on wholesale, haphazard, and uncritical borrowing. European thought, in the process of "translation" into the language of the Arab secular, liberal, or leftist intellectuals of the interwar period, underwent significant distortion. Trapped in the vocabulary of "newspaper" Arabic, the translated thought emerged in hardly recognizable form.

What I have termed naive thought is ideologically variable, defined less by concrete content than by form. Thus, for example, if the dominant discourse of the European period upheld the ideas and ideologies of liberalism, humanism, socialism, reason, progress, and so forth, this fact had little significance for the way Arab intellectuals conceptualized these doctrines or their concrete expressions. The social context daily belied the legitimacy or even credibility of these concepts. This abstract, largely idealistic approach to social reality rendered the intermediate intellectual generation an objective supporter of the status quo represented by both European domination and, later, the bourgeois rule of the early years of independence. The one-dimensional character of liberal intellectual discourse is apparent in the way it formulated its criticism: preaching and rhetoric, the identity of word and deed, was its secular mode of *action*.[21] This tendency emerges clearly in the manner of writing prevalent in the 1920s, 1930s, and 1940s. Whatever its specific content, the writing of this period tended toward formal principles and reinforced the dominant monological discourse. By its naive or utopian vision it obscured the social context of material reality and helped to cover up the horror of everyday life. It is not surprising that social practice when independence was achieved reflected not only a sharp divorce between ideology and practice but also abandonment of the prescriptions of theory or ideology (now reduced to pure rhetoric combined with *realpolitik*) toward naked activism and, finally, after the collapse of the ideological political parties (in the 1950s) and the rise of the modern sultanate state, toward pure Machiavellianism.

8

Radical Criticism
of Neopatriarchal Culture

The New Critics

The period of the 1970s and 1980s, which marks neopatriarchal society's highest material prosperity and the beginning
of its social and political stagnation, coincides with the emergence of an impressive body of scholarly and critical works
forming the first radical critique of neopatriarchy. Grounded
in the various disciplines of the humanities and social sciences, these writings are all inspired by modes of thinking
derived from three basic trends: critical Anglo-American social science, Western Marxism, and French structuralist and
post-structuralist thought.[1]

The mode and substance of this new critical movement was
foreshadowed by the avant-garde literary magazine *Mawaqif*
(Positions), published in Beirut beginning in 1968, in its first
editorial, written by Adonis.

> [*Mawaqif* speaks for] the generation that has experienced the dis-
> integration and paralysis of contemporary Arab society; a genera-
> tion determined to embark on a new search of discovery and re-
> building.
>
> *Mawaqif* seeks to be in the forefront [of this movement]. But to be
> in the vanguard means to be inventive, original—that is, to be on
> the offensive, willing and ready to destroy what is rejected and to
> replace it by what we wish to set up. Culture is creativity; it is not
> using tools, but inventing them. . . . It [should] symbolize the re-

jection of what we have inherited and what has come down to us, and what has been written for us and about us.

Culture from this standpoint is struggle, unity of thought and action, inventing the world, life and man, with this goal in mind: to change the world, and to transform life and man; a culture that is also a revolution.[2]

As pointed out earlier, by the end of the 1960s, neopatriarchal thought in its reformist, secularist, nationalist, and leftist modes had reached a cul-de-sac: the end of an epoch was now clearly visible. Such thought was unable to cope with either the inner (social) conflict or the pressures of the external (political) world, or to manage the opposition between "modernity" and "authenticity" (*asalah*), and thus slid back into religious defensiveness. Secularist doctrines (reformism, liberalism, socialism) had not been able to strike deep root in neopatriarchal soil, not so much because of their intrinsic inapplicability to Arab social structures, but because of the distortion to which these doctrines were subjected in their translation into neopatriarchal forms. It was finally clear that neopatriarchal thought had reached its limit.

Let us now briefly characterize the critical movement that arose to challenge this thought, and some of its representative writers. As a reading against the neopatriarchal text, the new criticism threatens to undermine the concepts, procedures, values, and assumptions of the hegemonic discourse on several levels. On the *linguistic* level, this critique aims directly to transform the vocabulary of the neopatriarchal discourse and to create a new terminology and language. On the *interpretive* level, it seeks to dismantle the dominant categories of interpretation, and to establish fresh perspectives from which to displace the limiting horizon of neopatriarchal understanding. On the *ideological* level, it aims to deconstruct ideological thought in its various forms and to open up dialogical "space": Finally, on the level of *social practice,* it seeks (albeit tentatively) to delegitimate the theoretical underpinnings of theological authority and political power. Language and linguistic reconstruction are central to this project, such that the cleansing and refinement of discursive terminology—the overcoming of *literalness* and of the *rhetorical* and *ideological* character of naive interpretation—are seen as the first tasks of criticism. The new language, as it has gradually emerged, has acquired independent purpose and rigor; it has no longer allowed the classical tongue to "speak itself"—to impose a literary or rhetorical mode—but has bent it into an increasingly effective vehicle for a rapidly maturing critical consciousness.

Thus, over the last two decades, the new critique has given rise to a new kind of discourse, one in which the appropriation of Western concepts and approaches—particularly those of the social sciences, Marxism, structuralism, feminism, and deconstruction—has become possible. The systematic questioning of ideological, religious, and fundamentalist thought became possible with the prospect of an independent *rereading* of history and society. The past was no longer to be constantly celebrated as a perfect, glorious heritage or utopian vision; and society was no more to be seen as embodying eternal values and unchangeable relations. Both were now projected into their specific, historical structures and rendered open to analysis and criticism.

The rereading offered by these critics for the first time challenged the unity of the neopatriarchal discourse in its basic foundations. Different interpretations already became available, produced from different standpoints by disciplined research and fresh analysis, legitimating further analysis and debate.

Perhaps the new criticism penetrated most deeply in those areas that were most closely guarded by the neopatriarchal discourse: the domains of the unthought (*impensé*) and the unsaid (*non-dit*)—of the body, of sexuality, or the generally prohibited. For in the new mode of discourse, customs, traditions, and rituals were no longer truths or values but clues, signs, and symbols disclosing meanings which neopatriarchal discourse sought to hide or distort—for example, the sexual question, the role of women, political power and sexual repression, and so forth. For reasons difficult to pin down briefly, the new interpretive approach was undertaken with particular effectiveness by North African intellectuals and scholars, particularly in Morocco, where the movement found its strongest and clearest expression.

The Critical Content

In the field of *scholarly* criticism the three most important Maghribi writers are represented by Muhammad 'Abed al-Jabiri, Muhammad Arkoun, and 'Abdallah Laroui. They were the first to develop, in the 1970s and early 1980s, new analytical perspectives from which radically new rereadings of history and society became possible.

Jabiri derives his categories directly from Michel Foucault, who bases his work on a clear distinction between the conventional "history of ideas" approach, with its notions of influence, sequence, accumulation, and so on, and the new "archeology of knowledge" with its emphasis on rupture, discontinuity, repetition, and so forth. Thus, Jabiri, by considering the "Arab mind" in terms of a *body* of thought and a *way* of thinking, is able to treat the former in terms of an "Arab specificity" and the latter as a product of certain "methods and ways of thought."[3] His project is on the one hand to "carry on the study of Arab Muslim culture" begun by various neopatriarchal scholars, and to "initiate," on the other, a new kind of investigation "to uncover the real structure of the Arab mind and its mechanisms."[4] He divides his project into two parts, "one dealing with the formation of the Arab mind, and the other with the analysis of the structure of the Arab mind—the first [to] be approached from a diachronic standpoint, and the other from a synchronic one."[5]

Muhammad Arkoun's concern is similar to Jabiri's, but narrower and therefore more focused. His aim is to break the monopoly of traditional and neopatriarchal interpretation of

the sacred and literary texts of Islamic culture.[6] He seeks to
do this by first establishing new ground for the (re)reading of
the Quran, a reading that would put aside philological and
orientalist methods and rely instead on the modern disciplines of linguistics, semiology, anthropology, sociology, and
history.[7] Such a new reading would not only displace the traditionalist perspective and provide a new conception of self
and the world, but would also free powers of critical understanding and analysis hitherto suppressed by the dominant
traditional (neopatriarchal) reading.

The condition for achieving the new reading lies in the
"difficult process" of establishing the validity of a secular
multidisciplinary approach to interpreting the Quran. In an
interview in 1984, following the publication of his major
work, *Pour une critique de la raison islamique,* Arkoun defined this problem as follows:

> Secularism involves taking an intellectual position with regard to
> two issues:
>
> The first is linked to the problem of knowledge. How can the mean-
> ing of events be grasped? How can we understand reality in an ac-
> curate and precise way? Is it not impermissible to deny anyone, for
> no matter what reason, the right to understand?
>
> The second is, how can we communicate knowledge after its dis-
> covery and crystalization? When we discover new results in any field
> of knowledge our responsibility to communicate these results is as
> important as their discovery. . . . I have personally experienced a
> great difficulty, and still do, with [communicating] my findings in
> the field of Islamic and Arab thought. It is a difficult problem.[8]

Arkoun has no illusions about overcoming this "difficult
problem," because it is not merely methodological but rooted
in political power and religious vested interest. He sees the
possibility of change only as part of a larger process of intellectual and linguistic transformation. For this to come about,
he maintains, the way thinking happens and the way language
articulates thought must first change. "Change must involve
the way in which reality is expressed in and by language. Lan-

guage must be changed, that is, it must be secularized and rationalized."[9]

'Abdallah Laroui was among the first Maghribi scholars to challenge the prevailing discourse. In his book on the crisis of the Arab intellectuals, he bitterly attacks the neopatriarchal discourse, which Arkoun seeks to dismantle by legitimating a "secular" reading of the Quran. Laroui denounces this discourse from another position, for its slavish *salafi* (traditionalist) and eclectic orientations, and for its confusion and ambivalence—which only lead to the "freedom of a stoic slave."[10] He sees this kind of "historical thinking" as having "but one consequence, failure to see the real."[11] This is why the (neopatriarchal) intellectuals are as impotent in dealing with social and political reality as in confronting Western thought *and* their own Islamic tradition. The only way out, according to Laroui, is basically the way suggested by Jabiri and Arkoun.

> The only way to do away with these two modes of thought is in strict submission to the discipline of historical thought and acceptance of all its assumptions . . . : truth as process, the positivity of the event, the determination of facts, the responsibility of the agents. Others delimit historicism: the existence of laws of historical development, the unity of the meaning of history, the transmissibility of acquired knowledge, the effectivity of the intellectual's and the politician's role.[12]

Laroui points out that "to believe in Providence" as do the *salafis,* or to be "constantly lapsing into the psychology of heroes of the past," or to fall as the eclectics do under "the mercy of every passing fashion," will only consolidate present alienation and reinforce the power of the dominant discourse. Laroui advocates Marxism as the "best school of historical thought . . . that the Arabs may find"—a Marxism, however, "read in a certain manner"[13]: presumably, in the manner in which most of the critical writers agree it should be read, that is, not as theology or political dogma, or a "Marxism-Leninism," but as a methodology and an analytical theory, a source of critical categories in the manner of Western Marxism.

Proceeding from the same sensitivity to the central episte-mological problem underlying the confrontation with neo-patriarchal thought, two leading Syrian Marxists, Sadiq al-'Azm and Elias Murqus, highlight in their Marxist critique two basic oppositions: the classical opposition between reli-gious and secular thought, and the more recently formulated opposition between thought and language.

'Azm, in his provocatively titled book, *Critique of Religious Thought,* confronts the religious world-view of neopatriar-chal society head-on, not merely as a traditional mode of reading and understanding, but as an alienating ideology in the service of a socially and intellectually oppressive status quo. In his polemical attack he uses the same rhetoric em-ployed by the Young Hegelians (and the young Marx), de-scribing religion as simply a means of estranging humanity from its own essence. 'Azm defines religious thought as

> nothing but the surface of a general amalgam of thoughts, percep-tions, beliefs, purposes, and [mental] habits we refer to by various names: "religious mentality," "*salafi* spiritualist mentality," and so forth. In this sense, the religious mentality is characterized by the prevalence of spontaneous acceptance of the conscious conformity of the dominant metaphysical ideology expressed in a tidy, consis-tent, and reasonable form.[14]

The thrust of his criticism is also directed as much at the producers of religious ideology, as at the secularist intellec-tuals who refuse or lack the nerve to confront this false con-sciousness.

> After the Arab defeat of 1967 a number of progressive Arab writers did confront certain aspects of the traditional social life, the intel-lectual structure, and the cultural legacy of contemporary Arab so-ciety. In most cases, however, their criticism was confined to the superstructural and superficial layers of society (thought, education, legislation, ideology) and consequently it was an impotent and anemic critique. . . . Most of it consisted of repetitions of clichés of familiar broad generalizations denouncing "dependent meta-physical mentality" and "belief in metaphysics, myths, and miracu-

lous solutions," and of appeals to the Arab people and its leaders to turn to the "scientific method" and to take up the rational approach.[15]

"None of these [progressive] critics," he adds,

> undertook to expose the metaphysical [religious] mentality by deal-·ing with it directly, analyzing in a rational and scientific way its concrete productions, its ideological claims and its interpretations of concrete events.[16]

'Azm's dissatisfaction with the more progressive neopatriarchal writers stems from his rejection of the neopatriarchal discourse in its religious as well as its secular form. For him only a radical Marxist critique, dispelling religious and political mystification, can undermine the prevailing (false) consciousness and pave the way for "constructing an entirely modern Arab society."[17]

'Azm's critique is perhaps the most daring confrontation of religious power undertaken since the beginning of the Awakening. By reducing the religious discourse to some of its social and political implications, and by linking these to the defeat of 1967, he was able to invest the Marxist critique with a concreteness unknown in the literature of the old Arab Left.

Though interested in the same issues, Elias Murqus' primary concern is the epistemological question and its linguistic and methodological implications. In an article published in 1984 in *al-Wihda* (*Unity*) entitled "The Problematic of Method: Modernizing or Founding," he accepts 'Azm's premises and goes beyond them. It is not enough (or even feasible) just to secularize existing (neopatriarchal) theoretical practice; a radical epistemological break (in the Althusserian sense) must be made not only with religious thought but with all forms of neopatriarchal thought. Murqus refuses to treat "prevailing thought" as proper *thought* and insists on defining it as a form of *fiqh* (scholastic, traditional thought). The *fiqh* paradigm governs not only religious (fundamentalist) thought but all thought in neopatriarchal society, including Marxist, liberal, and reformist thought. There is only "nationalist *fiqh*, Marxist *fiqh* . . . cultural *fiqh*."[18]

The epistemological break, according to Murqus, may take different forms, but to take root a transformation of consciousness must precede it, beginning with a transition from "symbolism and objectivism" to what he terms "conceptualism and realism," that is, from naive empiricism to philosophical self-consciousness.[19] This development is possible only when the parallel myths of petty bourgeois modernism and religious revivalism have been criticized, demystified, and abandoned. Murqus rejects abstract bourgeois thought, which replaces the "relation of signifier and signified with the relation of thought and reality,"[20] as vehemently as the thought of those who celebrate the unity of "religion and science."[21] Only Marxist thought which is neither "bourgeois progress [nor] a catching up with the West (the socialist project of world revolution)" can be genuinely "opposed to theology, metaphysics, and idealism" and can offer an authentic alternative: a "scientific theory" and a "scientific philosophy."[22]

Critical social science, particularly as developed since 1970 in England and the United States, represents another current, in which the epistemological problem is dealt with from an altogether different point of view. Here, too, the critical approach begins with rejection of ideological abstractions and insistence on an empirical, classificatory approach as, for example, Halim Barakat does in his pioneering study, *Contemporary Arab Society*.

> Here I will seek to analyze social phenomena in their proper social context, and in their relations and interrelations, unlike the abstract and absolutist approach. I will emphasize the national and social contradictions within society as well as the nature of the social and political struggles that aim to resolve these contradictions.[23]

The Egyptian social scientist, Saad al-Din Ibrahim, suggests the areas on which such an empirical approach should be focused: "the human base," "the ecological base," "class structure," "ethnic structures," "formal institutions," "value systems and Arab behavioral patterns," "origin and structure of the Arab state," "the nation state," "Arab ruling elites," "problems of political participation," and "problems of political and social stability."[24]

Structuralism provides still another approach to dealing with the epistemological problem. Kamal Abu Dib, a leading Syrian structuralist critic, describes this approach in the introduction to his ground-breaking book, whose intent he describes as at once "revolutionary and founding, rejectionist and oppositional."[25]

> Structuralism is not a philosophy, but a way of seeing and a method of dealing with reality. Structuralism does not change language or society or poetry. But in its rigor and insistence on fundamental analysis, on multi-dimensional understanding and the pursuit of the real determinants of things as well as the relations between them, it changes thought—in the way it deals with language and society and poetry—and transforms it into a questioning, doubting, pursuing, seeking, comprehending, dialectical thought.[26]

The post-structuralist or deconstructive approach is best represented by Abdelkebir Khatibi and his Moroccan followers. His book, *La blessure du nom propre*,[27] is particularly important; it represents perhaps the most incisive and original critique of neopatriarchal thought to appear in the last two decades.

In the words of Muhammad Benniss, Khatibi's translator and principal interpreter, Khatibi's project is an attempt at

> a critical rereading of the Arab body in the light of popular Moroccan Arab culture. . . . This rereading seeks to distinguish between the body as abstract concept and the body as experienced in terms of concrete, lived reality.

> Arab [neopatriarchal] culture deals with the body only abstractly, tying it to the theological principles which empty it of all historical and subjective weight.

He adds:

> The discourse of contemporary [neopatriarchal] culture is essentially a discourse of books about books, whether it deals with rereading the Arab tradition or with confronting the historical present . . . [that is,] class difference, linguistic difference, historical difference, geographical difference, and all the [other] differences contemporary cultural discourse has sought to suppress. . . . Here, in Khatibi's text, Nietzsche, Heidegger, Marx, Freud, Levi-Strauss, Lacan and Derrida are able to speak.[28]

Khatibi's perspective is formed by Roland Barthes' semiology and Jacques Derrida's deconstruction, which he uses to subvert the sway of the absolutist theo-ideological concepts of neopatriarchal thought.[29] As he sees it, the first step in this direction is to "deconstruct the Arab sociological categories derived from mainstream Western sociology," to unmask the "self-centered ideology of Western philosophy and social science."[30] This should be accomplished within Arab sociological "writing and knowledge," as a self-criticism that would measure the extent of its own dependency on Western paradigms in this writing and knowledge, and at the same time would reveal the self-reflective character of these paradigms. Thus in Khatibi's critique what is put into question is not just "traditional" knowledge but the "rational" and "modern" writing of Arab secular writers and scholars, including the work of some of his fellow critics.[31] He considers this writing "alien to itself" and unable to resolve, let alone locate and properly identify, its problematic—an interlocking struggle between two systems of knowledge in which one system dominates the other.

> The Arab scholar or man of science is the translator and articulator of a methodological and theoretical body of knowledge that has been formed in a different language and in other countries; in most cases, he hardly understands the historical and philosophical ground of this body of knowledge. He feels crushed by the scientific production of the Other . . . and is satisfied to remain in the shadow of Western knowledge and to formulate a secondary knowledge of his own. . . . However, everything will be shaken on the level of theory when we become aware of this tension, and when the Arab world puts a stop to the process of accumulation and concentrates

instead on establishing the conditions and requirements of its own [independent] production; at that point it will become clear that everything must start anew from the very beginning. This means that when [the Arab world] has properly mastered Western knowledge it will see that the matter does not call for just adopting and translating this knowledge but also and at the same time analyzing and comprehending the process of its formation, transformation, and break in the course of history.[32]

According to Khatibi, it is not *ignorance* that accounts for the confusions and contradictions of neopatriarchal thought; on the contrary, "the Arab world has become so thoroughly imbued with Western knowledge that it no longer knows what position to take or where the source of the problems that plague it lies."[33]

Another step to be taken in order to dismantle the established mode of discourse involves the rejection of "historicism" and preoccupation with the past. A new "critical practice" is needed "that would define our being here and now"[34] and be carried out "in relation to what was termed by an Egyptian sociologist 'a rationality with multiple variables.' "[35] Such a critical practice or reading would "shake the very ground on which the dominant [neopatriarchal] system of knowledge now stands."[36]

If we implement this project we shall clear the ground for a new writing. Of course, a new writing could not be completed overnight, but with infinite patience we would be able to undo the theoretical chains that bind us inside and out. This is no doubt an endless project. We all know that where [authentic] knowledge is concerned there is no place for miracles, only for critical breaks.[37]

As Muhammad Benniss points out in his introduction to Khatibi's *La blessure du nom propre,* Khatibi's whole project proceeds from a distinction between "the *conceptual* and the *real* body of society" (italics added),[38] implying an epistemological move suggested by none of his fellow critics: he calls for a fundamental shift from a thought grounded in general concepts and totalizing theory to one focusing on the particu-

lar, the historical, and the concrete, that is, on humanity as
body, on "desire" and "pleasure" as central categories of analysis.[39] In the kind of writing Khatibi suggests, concepts such
as "difference," "margin," and "other" would replace identity, center, and totality, and would provide a new perspective, more advanced than that put forth by any of the other
new critics. Thus his critique has a subversive radicalism lacking in most of the writings of the radical writers, including
those of the Left.

> Some Arab Marxists maintain that if we change the infrastructure
> and the mode of power in the Arab countries, the ideological super-
> structure will sooner or later also change. They believe that Marx-
> ism is the only way to achieve a break with underdevelopment and
> religious oppression. But when we carefully examine this assertion
> we soon realize that this simplified Marxism will only again lead us
> to theology. Marxism will overcome theology only when the ques-
> tion of difference becomes the focus of authentic thought in the
> world. And until this is realized, we should teach Marxism and dis-
> seminate it with great care.[40]

The Foreignness of the New Critics

Ibn Khaldun, the medieval Arab "sociologist," deploring the
depressed state of learning in his time (the fifteenth century),
makes the following observation: "The strange thing is that
nowadays most Muslim scholars [i.e., intellectuals] are non-
Arab. . . . Those few who are Arab, are so only by descent,
for they are foreign in their language, upbringing and education.[41]

This description most aptly fits the Western-educated intellectuals I refer to as the radical or modern or new critics of
the 1970s and 1980s.[42] Most of these intellectuals may be
characterized as "foreign" in the sense intended by Ibn Khaldun, that is, they are "foreign" not by religion or nationality,
but because of their education and culture—their different
way of thinking, speaking, and writing.

The language of the new critics, from Sadiq al-'Azm and

Muhammad Arkoun to Abdelkebir Khatibi and Muhammad Benniss, is thus foreign in both a figurative and literal sense. In the literal sense, for most members of this group the primary language of expression is English or French; even if they have total command of Arabic (as many of them do not), their primary mode of discourse derives from one of these two languages. This linguistic duality has important cultural and epistemological consequences for the character of the radical critics and the new critical discourse; this duality is immediately evident when we consider the sharp distinction between the Latin-French and Anglo-American cultures, in temper, sensibility and modes of thought and perception. The new critics have been absorbed by their education, training, and experience in the direction of one or the other of these two cultures. As such they constitute two subgroups, one Anglo-American-oriented, the other French-oriented, relating to one another not merely as Arabs (or Muslims) but as French or American-trained intellectuals: they see one another in terms of "translations" which the French and the Anglo-Americans make of each other as cultures or discourses or texts. In other words, to a large extent these two subgroups relate to other cultures and traditions, including their own, through the knowledge, methods, and concepts with which these two Western cultures understand themselves, each other, and the rest of the world.[43]

The figurative sense in which the language of this new breed of Arab intellectuals may be considered foreign is that their kind of Arabic (in writing, whether their own or in translation) is hardly comprehensible, not only to the ordinary reader but to the typical neopatriarchal intellectual as well. What makes the radical critics' language (Khatibi's for example) so difficult to understand is not only its peculiar terminology and style, but the logical and formal structures in which it gets expressed. In the new discourse the ground has changed: familiar Arabic terms no longer have the same significations, traditional forms are mixed and disrupted, and known stylistic conventions are neglected or ignored. Here a modern Arabic weighted with new content and producing a genuinely critical text may be said to have begun to emerge. This new language can do what its traditional or neopatriarchal variants (classical and "newspaper" Arabic) cannot hope to accomplish: confront the Western discourse on its own terms and interact with it critically—antagonistically—on a level of cognitive parity.

We must clearly distinguish therefore between the group of intellectuals we have termed the new critics and the generality of contemporary intellectuals (the "educated")—including graduates of Western-style or European and American universities. Since the end of World War II, tens of thousands of Arab students have studied abroad and managed to obtain advanced degrees in the sciences and humanities. Yet it can be argued that these "educated" have remained unchanged in their basic intellectual and "linguistic" orientations, and have maintained, except for the acquisition of certain professional expertise, the outlook and mode of thought characteristic of their neopatriarchal upbringing and background—whether in conservative, reformist, or secular form.

On the other extreme, within the group of new critics there is a small minority of intellectuals, mostly expatriates, who stand apart by virtue of their having been wholly absorbed into their Western milieu or having become fully Westernized—without, however, losing their inner identity or commitment. Most of these individuals were born or raised in the West and acquired a distinctly Western quality of thought and speech. From their standpoint, which truly bridges the cultural and psychological divide between West and non-West, neopatriarchal society appears as an external totality, thus as approachable from the "outside," "objectively," "scientifically." Together with other expatriates, mostly those teaching in European and American universities, this Westernized minority constitutes a critical force of increasing influence. As the expatriate intellectuals of the early phase of the Awakening did not, this group now has at its disposal the means of significantly influencing the debate abroad, among the expatriate community, as well as in the Arab world.

As for the new critics living in the Arab world, they are numerically the largest group among the new critical intellectuals, consisting mostly of graduates of French, American, or British universities, with a strong grasp of the methodologies and problematics in their own disciplines (social sciences and humanities). Their particular effectiveness derives from two sources: a strong command of the new critical "language" and its intellectual ground, as well as close familiarity with the sources and traditions of Islam and Arab literature and history. Their limitation is produced by the conditions under which they live—the political, ideological, and economic conditions characteristic of the contemporary neopatriarchal status quo, with its limitations on freedom of thought and criticism.

Contact between the new critics in the Arab world and those living in the West has considerably increased since the late 1970s, and between the two groups some concrete forms of cooperation have evolved—for example, in the founding of independent professional associations and human rights and women's organizations, and the convening of pan-Arab conferences devoted to the discussion of social and cultural issues. As these links grow stronger and the modes of cooperation and organization continue to increase, the new criticism looms more and more as a serious threat to the dominant neopatriarchal discourse. Let us now assess this threat and its possible effect on social and political outcomes.

Criticism and Creativity

The first consideration we must take into account is that the radical critics should be regarded more as *methodologists* than as *theoreticians,* for they have been engaged more in promoting a critical approach than in devising an original theory.

Thus the radical critique derives its effectiveness not so much from discovery as from acquired modes of analysis and interpretation. And so the Arab writers and scholars engaged in the new cultural criticism may be termed second-degree critics, for none of them can be properly regarded as a truly *creative* or *original* historian, philosopher, sociologist, or literary critic. Even their most advanced output is still largely negative, concerned with *problematizing* rather than *theorizing* their subject matter. Inasmuch as criticism and synthesis fall short of truly theorizing thought, the radical critique, despite its qualitative difference from all neopatriarchal criticism since the beginning of the Awakening, represents only a first stage of autonomous self-consciousness.

Criticism as such may be considered only the first level of a process of which *synthesis* (autonomous perspective, coherence, unity) and *creativity* (independent vision, original theory, "going beyond") form the higher levels, and the critical movement must embrace these levels to achieve genuine and independent self-consciousness. The following table specifies the levels of conscious thought.

Modernity (Active)	Neopatriarchy (Reactive)
Criticism	Tradition
Synthesis	Dependency
Creativity	Imitation

Thus, on the first level, the critical movement consists of a double critique directed both at the Self and the Other, in a project aimed at displacing the neopatriarchal discourse by dismantling the Western *and* patriarchal frameworks in which it is enclosed. The next step would be a unifying synthesis, then a creative theory—at those two levels, the contestation of the Self and Other enter the framework of modernity.

But even on the primary (critical) level, the new critics confront difficulties they seem unable to resolve. For example, they face the persistence of the (invisible) Western categories and codes, which penetrate their ways of thought and expression, providing the secret or implicit model of their self-evaluation. There seems to be no way around the West, the antagonistic Other which they seek to dismantle and transcend but which constantly returns as the "culture of reference" (Derrida), positing itself as *universally* valid.[44] Thus Hegel and Marx, Durkheim and Weber, Nietzsche and Freud, Althusser and Foucault fashion the paradigms which not only govern European thought but subordinate and absorb all intellectual production everywhere else: to think is to think in Western forms. What kind of critique can displace the claims of such self-universalizing thought? What methodology is required to historicize and delimit it? What kind of approach would make for interaction and exchange with it without antagonism or subordination?

Another difficulty the modern critical movement faces has to do with the problem of "translation"—making the transition from one paradigm to another, rendering one cognitive system intelligible in terms of another.[45] This problematic may be illustrated by the question: How can society, history, change, consciousness, be independently theorized? Is this possible by means of "translated" categories? A further question: What kind of understanding is achieved by borrowed or acquired intuitions? How, for instance, can Marx or Derrida be grasped "in Arabic?"

Translation (of the Western discourse) thus involves, in turn, a double alienation, linguistic and paradigmatic. The linguistic alienation can be immediately grasped as the contradiction of a *classical* language reproducing a *modern* text. The paradigmatic question, on the other hand, lies in the ultimate impossibility of complete correspondence between different cognitive systems. Hence the puzzling question: What does it mean (what is it) to be a cultural and linguistic outsider reading the Western text from the outside?[46]

This central dilemma has always been faced in two fundamentally different ways: from the secularist position and the traditionalist position. While the former persists in affirming such categories in the Western discourse as "reason," "science," "humanity," or "democracy," the latter rejects the alien discourse altogether and insists on its replacement by the traditional text. Neither is able to overcome the essential foreignness of the Western discourse.

It may be that only radical gestures, similar to one suggested by the traditionalist position but in the opposite direction—that is, total immersion in the Western discourse—might make it possible to grasp the foreign text from within, and thus to approach neopatriarchal reality neither as an alien Other nor as a defensive Self (i.e., neither from the position of external dependence nor of internal submission), but as a reality *in and for itself*. And this kind of break, I think, is largely what the new critics who are concerned with deconstructing the neopatriarchal discourse seem to aim at. So far, however, their writing remains disjointed and incomplete, lacking a coherent, systematic character. For one thing, this writing is shaped by concerns related not only to their own society and culture, but also to living and professional survival in alien environments. And, while the issues may be approached "politically" by the critics living in the Arab countries, their Westernized and expatriate colleagues may approach these same issues in "objective" or "theoretical" ways, in the framework more of Western "universal" thought than of politics and commitment.

Another difficulty is generated by the new critics' (living both in and outside the Arab world) own *didactic* mode of discourse, which necessarily delimits the horizon of theory by often imposing prescriptive considerations. Such practice not only bends theory to adjust to practical concerns (to what Jameson calls the "narrowly political horizon"), but also risks losing sight of the appropriate theoretical formulations, when the latter refer to areas beyond practical or political concerns.

The distinction between "prescriptive" (didactic) and "ob-

jective" approaches seems never to have been so absent or
unimportant as it is to the neopatriarchal intellectuals and
"educated" strata, who seem always to assume that Western
universalist concepts, procedures, theories, and so forth, could
simply be transferred in the way Western products are transferred—selectively and at will. They seem unable to see the
necessity of the vital separation between the recipients' psychic economy and material being and the conditions of cultural production of the conceptual systems imported by them.
The new radical critics, on the other hand, though quite
aware of the distinction, still have to address its implications.
This gap is evident, for example, in that their tone is rhetorical and they are more concerned to insert borrowed concepts
and methods in their discourse than to explain and ground
this discourse in intelligible "Arab" terms. Thus, for example, Jabiri's Foucaultian archeology, Khatibi's Barthesian semiotics and Benniss's Derridan deconstruction tend to be
inserted directly into the new language without proper "translation"—a fact which has tended to narrow this critical circle
and encourage trendy Western forms of thought and interpretation.

In conclusion, I should perhaps say a word concerning the
role of structuralist and post-structuralist criticism, perhaps
the most incisive in the current movement of Arab radical
criticism. The significance of this perspective lies in its devastating effectiveness in undermining privileged positions from
within the neopatriarchal discourse, in displacing monological
authority, in opening up to genuine pluralism, and in recognizing excluded and degraded positions (minorities, women).
But this project has another side to it which suffers certain
limitations in the Arab political and ideological setting.

In the first place, the immanent and formalistic orientation
of structuralism and deconstruction tends to shut off political
and practical relevancies and to focus on language and tex-
tuality, thus running the risk of turning attention away from
political reality. What is the point of *naming* the oppressed,

the marginalized, the humiliated, if the enterprise stops at an abstract *gesture?* The point must be made that if the context of an institutionally centralized society (such as Derrida's France) needs a detotalizing thrust, that thrust loses its significance where, as in Arab neopatriarchal society, the context on the contrary requires a totalizing movement (to unify fragmented opposition).[47] Similarly with the problem of "anarchism." If, in the context of late industrial society, post-structuralist anarchism provides the illusion of the play of freedom and plurality, the primary need in authoritarian neopatriarchal society goes beyond anarchism's delight in deconstructive plays—as carried out, for example, by Khatibi and Benniss. Without a comprehensive theory, deconstructive criticism ends up being a fragmented project unable to provide clear political purpose. This apolitical stance, though making it possible to evade the direct censorship and material strictures of neopatriarchal authority, is bound to push deconstructive criticism more and more in the direction of an individualistic "ideology of desire" and away from a collective ideology of social and political struggle. How, finally, can an authentic criticism, carried out in a social context of oppression, ferment, and upheaval, do away (as does deconstructive criticism) with the category of totality: history, society, people, class, nation? Specifically, how is it possible to deal with the all-inclusive phenomenon of neopatriarchy without a coherent approach to history and society? It should not be surprising therefore if sometimes even some of the most acute among the new critics should seem to leave empty the space where political revolution appears as an unconditional necessity.

9

The Final Phase

Petty Bourgeois Hegemony

The third quarter of the twentieth century (the postindependence period) saw the maturation of a social process that had its origins in the interwar period: the transformation of neopatriarchal society into a *mass* society. Now the social structure of neopatriarchal society began to assume the character of a mass—made up, however, not of proletarians or peasants and workers in a clear sense[1] but of a featureless amalgam, best expressed in Lenin's observation about Czarist Russia before the revolution, a transitional society at the point of internal disintegration: "There is no people—yet there is a mass of people."

In Arab neopatriarchal society, this "mass of people," this social structure without distinct class differentiation or class consciousness, was the result of petty bourgeois hegemony. By 1970, the petty bourgeoisie had grown in size and importance sufficiently to occupy center stage in social and political life. The other two classes, the bourgeoisie and the working class, remained undeveloped; that is, neither developed into full-fledged classes capable of seizing or maintaining social or political dominance.[2]

The working class never escaped the effects of dependent development and remained small and weak, both in structure and political influence. The underdevelopment of the working class and the bourgeoisie is also closely linked to the process of urbanization alluded to above, which bolstered petty bourgeois power and brought it to political and social ascendancy.[3] A crucial factor in this process is the persistence of subsistence farming (even after the introduction of land reform) which greatly increased the emigration to cities—swelling the ranks of the jobless and the semi-employed and, equally important, keeping alive the values and traditions of the oral rural culture which prevented the crystallization of a properly proletarian culture or consciousness.[4]

It is essential that we understand the nature and role of the neopatriarchal petty bourgeoisie if we are to attain a proper grasp of social and political developments in the postindependence period. Recall that the petty bourgeoisie, originating as it does in both city and countryside, is in fact a hybrid class linked culturally and socially to its peasant and bourgeois origins, forming a kind of historical outgrowth of the conditions of external and internal dependency. Economically, it is a nonproductive class, strongly oriented toward consumer capitalism.[5] Its position in the productive process is peripheral and parasitical and its values and social relations are traditional, accounting in part for its ideological ambivalence and unstable social and political orientation. The neopatriarchal ethos is nowhere more strongly or clearly expressed than in the petty bourgeoisie: in it are simultaneously projected and magnified all the contradictions of neopatriarchy—between tradition and modernity, religion and secularism, capitalism and socialism, production and consumption. None of these contradictions can find resolution in this culture, which seems endlessly to generate conditions of conflict and debility, leading it to apparently inevitable collapse.

The political breakthrough of the petty bourgeoisie, which occurred in the 1950s with the coming to power of the young army officers and ideological nationalist parties, brought to an end the period of liberalism and reform and inaugurated the era labeled "revolutionary" by its ideologues. The landed and commercial bourgeoisie was dispossessed and expelled from political power (and, in large numbers, from the country), while the proletarian and semiproletarian strata were assimilated into the new social order, giving it its mass character. More gradually, the old intellectual elite gave way and was replaced by the new petty bourgeoisie intelligentsia which now dominated the cultural scene, on both the "high culture" and mass level.[6] But first we must briefly consider the social and political achievements of the petty bourgeoisie as a dominant class in the "revolutionary era."

The Petty Bourgeois "Revolution"

Once in power, the petty bourgeoisie aimed at nothing less, at least rhetorically, than the total reshaping of society. Significantly, in every case the new leadership, upon taking power, declared itself for socialism, unity, and independence (for ending all forms of dependency). All "revolutionary" regimes adopted the noncapitalist path of modernization, which meant rejecting the capitalist model advocated by Western theorists and pursuing a socialist model. Thus in the crucial decades of the 1950s and 1960s neopatriarchal society saw two competing approaches to social change and political organization, the "revolutionary" and the conservative; the former was dominant, and seemed to represent the wave of the future, or at least, the aggressive force of the times. The social and economic failure of the revolution by the early 1970s led not to the victory of capitalism and its mode of development (it too failed in achieving capitalist "modernization"), but to a sharpening of neopatriarchal society's contradictions and a speeding-up of the process of internal conflict.

Why and how did this failure occur?

To the young officers (and their ideological political partners) the capitalist path to modernization was unacceptable in principle. They rejected its dictum, "grow now, redistribute later," in favor of a revolutionary strategy whose slogan was "first get the social structure right."[7] They were impelled in their attitude by fear of the new colonialism, freshly embodied in the violent implantation of Israel on Arab soil, by the polarization of the Middle East between the two superpowers, and by an ideology oriented toward the goals of unity, independence, and social justice. The new ruling class, coming as it did from mostly modest or impoverished rural and small-town backgrounds, had no commercial interests to protect (as did the old bourgeoisie), and found it easy to equate national humiliation, economic exploitation, poverty, and so on with capitalism, liberalism, and conservative ideology. Still, neither Marxism nor Eastern communism presented itself as an alternative system or ideology. The "revolution" settled down to normal daily routine, becoming another Arab regime; the new military-political-bureaucratic leadership congealed into a new upper class, and the new society oriented itself more toward consumption than socialism, attracted more to Western materialism and consumer capitalism than to Soviet or Third World socialism. More and more the "revolution" found itself sliding back to nonsocialist and capitalist practices, and political repression.

For a while, however, the march toward a form of socialist transformation had seemed secure; by the mid-1960s the four most important countries of the Arab world, Egypt, Syria, Iraq, and Algeria—with over eighty-five percent of the population and possessing most of the region's strategic and natural resources—appeared committed to the socialist (or at least noncapitalist) road and to positive neutrality. The significance of this situation was such as to make the Arab "socialist" countries in Soviet eyes more important to the future of the Third World than either Cuba or Vietnam. For example, V. Solodovnikov and V. Bogoslovsky, writing in the early 1970s, portrayed Abdul Nasser's achievements as convincing confirmation of Lenin's views on the socialist transformation of the colonial countries of Asia and Africa.

The Arab Republic of Egypt occupies a special place among the developing countries of the East that have embarked on the road of progressive development and have proclaimed the building of a socialist society as the general goal of all deep-going socio-economic changes. It was the first among the countries of the Middle East and Africa to break off the chains of colonialism. The victory on July 23, 1952, of the national revolutionary forces, headed by Nasser, marked the beginning of an anti-imperialist, anti-feudal revolution that was to affect every aspect of the life of this Arab country.[8]

The theory of noncapitalist development stemmed from Lenin's conviction that the backward countries of Asia and Africa in the age of imperialism could progress to socialism without going through the stage of capitalism. This theory envisaged a movement of three basic stages: in the first stage, "national liberation," national independence replaces foreign rule; in the second stage, "national-democratic" transformation, social and economic development leads to the democratization of leadership and the erection of socialist institutions; and in the third stage, "socialist revolution," the national-democratic transformation develops into a socialist revolution.[9]

For the successful transition to socialism Lenin assumed that four basic conditions would obtain: (1) a special role for the peasants and the Communist Party, (2) a progressive role for the nationalist democrats, (3) the transformation (at a later stage) of the national democratic parties to Marxist parties, and (4) the continuous acceleration of noncapitalist development.[10]

But by the 1970s, contrary to these expectations, it was clear that the socialist project, initiated by the "revolutionary" petty bourgeois leadership, would not be fulfilled in any of its aspects. Socialism on the Leninist model was not likely to take root anywhere except in Southern Yemen (one of the least populous and most impoverished and isolated countries in the Arab world).[11]

In retrospect the causes for this failure appear clear-cut and may briefly be outlined as follows:

1. The social and economic fragmentation of the neopatriarchal Arab world. What nationalist theory or wishful thinking explicitly assumed—a single Arab fatherland, a united Arab nation—was negated by political practice and economic reality, and by state sovereignty and the priority given state interests over pan-Arab interests, whether by the conservative or "revolutionary" regimes.

2. The exposure and vulnerability, resulting from disunity and polarization, of these states (particularly the "revolutionary" ones) to direct military intervention by the Western powers and Israel—for example, Egypt under Nasser—and the emergence of economically crushing and politically dominant military establishments in the central Arab countries.

3. The dispersal and relative isolation of the bulk of the population, and its alienation from the state and any form of political participation—particularly the rural population and the semi-nomadic tribes. These conditions rendered the countryside somewhat immune to effective mobilization and indoctrination by nationalist or left ideology.[12]

4. The theoretical and political underdevelopment of Arab Marxism.

5. The misuse of oil power (e.g., for reinforcing state sovereignty over pan-Arabism) and its radically disruptive effect on the political economy of the Arab world.

The Subjective Factor

The character of the neopatriarchal petty bourgeoisie may most clearly be seen in the modes of behavior and attitude typical of its ruling elite, political leaders, ideologues, bureaucrats, army officers, and technocrats, who dominate social, political, economic, and cultural life. These behavioral and attitudinal structures are the expressions, in various forms, of the oral, monological culture of the neopatriarchal petty bourgeois regimes.

Work, a centrality in rural life, for example, has hardly a place in this elite's practice: work has no ethical or socially significant meaning, being neither a fulfillment of duty nor a means of self-fulfillment and objectification. For the typical bureaucrat, for instance, the workplace (one's office) is no more than an extension of the place of sociability and relaxation. There is little qualitative difference between what goes on in the office or what goes on in the salon, living room, or *diwan*. In all these places guests are received and entertained, coffee or tea served, and amiable conversation enjoyed at leisure. This is not just a pattern of local behavior, but an institutionally embodied and socially prevalent practice. Thus bureaucracy—in government, the military, education, business—projects a modernized exterior, but internally its structure is essentially patriarchal, animated by an elaborate system of personal relations, kinship, and patronage. These are all neopatriarchal institutions.

In this culture, personal concerns always take priority over institutional interests; between the private world (of family or self) and the community or society, the former's values and goals always come first. Though the social good (of society, the fatherland) is set up publicly as the highest ideal or goal, in actual social practice it hardly exists as an inner directing influence. Self-assertion, personal security, and the pursuit of private interest leave little (besides verbal) energy for servicing the public good or carrying out social duty. Patronage, based as it is on fear and greed, generates egoism and cynicism as it reinforces the system of obedience, passivity, and submission. What is the point of self-exertion or selfless labor when performance mostly goes unrecognized and unrewarded, and when getting ahead and being recognized depends upon personal relations, connections, and proper backing rather than competence, efficiency, hard work, or sacrifice? Is it surprising if under these circumstances the strategy of cultivating proper connections and investing in personal alliances should seem wiser and more effective than any amount of work or achievement? What one *is* in this neopatriarchal petty bourgeois world derives not from what one does or creates, but rather from the position one occupies, the title one carries, the connection or protection one enjoys. Public office is a privilege and public service a favor, as 'Abdullah Laroui writes:

> Public office (is) a privilege rather than a position of public service. Official relations are based on charity and loyalty . . . and the public officials' behavior is determined by private concerns in dealing with individuals who seek their official services.[13]

It is not difficult to see why cooperation and collective effort are hard to achieve, or how under these conditions social energy, instead of being concentrated in purposive action, gets diverted into personal benefit or sublimated into gossip, conspiracy, or sudden violence.

It may safely be maintained that the failure of the revolution was a foregone conclusion. There was no way for petty bourgeois nationalism to develop into Marxism; a vacillating, ideologically ambivalent leadership could not carry out *radical* social transformation. Even in the most "revolutionary" regimes the masses remained politically alienated and socially conservative. Instead of pursuing Marxist theory the leadership formulated its own neopatriarchal version of socialism, one which, not surprisingly, resisted the idea of class and class conflict and replaced it with the ideology of national unity and harmonious coexistence between classes under the benevolent rule of the Leader (father, patriarch).[14]

The nation as family, a metaphor very dear to Arab rulers—revolutionary, conservative, and semi-tribal alike—is the trans-ideological model of authority common to all neopatriarchal regimes, regardless of ideology or socioeconomic system. To mobilize the masses was as difficult or impossible in revolutionary regimes as in the conservative ones; the same authori-

tarian vertical relations existed everywhere, preventing genuine social integration and keeping the majority of the
population outside the mainstream of social and political life.
By the late 1960s the structural differences distinguishing
revolutionary from conservative or nonrevolutionary regimes
had virtually dissolved. Like the conservative societies, the
"revolutionary" petty bourgeois regimes were already strati-
fied into economically and politically differentiated social
groups, with the upper crust of a minority elite holding the
wealth and power, a thin middle stratum, and a broad lower
mass with layers encompassing the underprivileged, impoverished, and powerless majority. The lowest layers consisted of
alienated urban and rural masses that inhabited "revolutionary" and nonrevolutionary societies alike. Above all, the social
relations of neopatriarchy, especially patronage, were everywhere dominant.

It is not surprising that neither the socialist nor the capitalist mode of modernization should "take" in this hybrid
social formation. In its present stage, probably its final one
now beginning, we can see the early signs of both economic
disintegration and social and political unraveling. Let us deal
first briefly with the economic aspect, then the more complex
sociopolitical one.

The main features of economic disintegration are described
by Samir Amin in his book *The Arab Economy Today*.[15] His
conclusion may be summarized as follows:

1. By the 1980s the economic structure of the Arab countries,
   both conservative and progressive, had become more ex-
   ternally oriented than that of any group of countries in the
   Third World. Taken as a whole the Arab world by 1980
   had become the most fully integrated (i.e., dependent) region in the contemporary world system.[16]
2. Reliance during this period on imports of foodstuffs
   reached in the Arab world a level higher than in any other
   Third World region—thirty-three percent in value terms.

(Third World average was less than ten percent.) Food imports increased from $2 billion in 1970 to over $20 billion in 1980.[17]

3. Despite the availability of vast capital, import-substitution industrialization remained weak and desultory, less advanced than in Latin America. The continuing decline in agricultural production only served to increase dependence on the world system.[18]

4. The poorer half of the population was limited to less than a quarter of total consumption. Whatever "development" had been achieved in the preceding two or three decades, the truly poor had benefited little from it. "Reforms and development reduced inequalities *amongst the upper strata* but have done little to change the overall ratio between these strata and the really poor." (Italics added.)[19]

5. The ratio of surplus consumption of the privileged strata was inordinate: in 1976, for example, 37.7 percent of total labor (as compared to 9.6 percent in 1971 in France) was expended on the production of such surplus.[20] Qualified labor (a "scarce resource") was squandered in serving the privileged strata rather than fulfilling the basic needs of the mass of the population.[21]

6. Domination by the multinationals meant corresponding technological dependency. The Arab world imported virtually all its industrial means of production and depended more and more for its agricultural development on multinational agribusiness.[22] By the early 1980s the economy of the Arab world had become a disabled one, characterized by disjointed industrial development, backwardness in agricultural development, growing consumerism and widening inequality in income distribution, growing distortion of development orientation and the increasing waste of human and natural resources.[23]

7. Oil wealth, which rose astronomically after 1973, served only to aggravate distorted development, give life to semi-

tribal authority, and strengthen economic, military, and cultural dependency on the West. As Amin notes, the *illusion* of wealth created by oil had the same effect on the Arab world as the gold of the New World had on Spain in the seventeenth century; "it delay[ed] the fundamental changes that are necessary for any genuine renaissance."[24]

The Fundamentalism of the Petty Bourgeoisie

Ironically, from the moment it gained political power in the 1950s, the petty bourgeoisie began to split as a class. This division took place along political and economic lines, with the political, bureaucratic, military, and commercial elite forming the ruling segment, and the small government workers, shopkeepers, school teachers, artisans, and urban and rural producers making up the underlying mass. The more dominant the petty bourgeoisie became as a social group, the more concentrated the ruling elite became, and the larger and more proletarianized the petty producers and distributors. Revolution from above, bogged down in the political and economic realities of dependency and underdevelopment, not only failed to build the new society or unite the Arab nation but created its own social and ideological contradictions and brought about the inescapable conditions of its own decline. By the late 1960s rulers and ruled had already become polarized, divided by a collapse of trust: power lost its legitimacy, and social relations inclined more and more toward further patronage, control, suppression, and coercion. The balance between consensus and coercion tipped inexorably toward the latter as the legitimacy of ruler, regime, and ideology disintegrated.

Islamic fundamentalism emerges in the midst of this moral and political decline as the true ideology of salvation for the frustrated, alienated petty bourgeois mass and its proletarian extension. For the first time in a hundred years, fundamentalist Islam has found its appropriate class vehicle. The uprooted petty commodity producers and distributors and the proletarianized small bourgeoisie, rather than being propelled forward toward secular or revolutionary radicalism, are pulled back to their religious roots. Formulated in moral and corresponding political categories, Islamic fundamentalism expresses mass sentiment and belief as no nationalist or socialist ideology has been able to do up till now.

Islamic fundamentalism has always formed a strong current in the social and political life of neopatriarchal society but before now has never constituted a *dominant* one. From the early days of the Awakening, fundamentalism followed quietly in the wake of Islamic reformism, which until World War I served as the central ideological force in political life. While reformist ideas found their expression in the writings of some of the most brilliant figures of this period—Afghani, 'Abdu, Qassim Amin, and al-Kawakibi—conservative or fundamentalist Islam was represented by the traditionalist clergy and the old religious establishment. In the interwar period, as the reformist current began to recede, and liberal and nationalist thought replaced it, a different brand of fundamentalism began to arise, particularly after the founding of the Muslim Brothers in the early 1930s, which produced under its founder, Hassan al-Banna (d. 1949), the first fully articulated *political* program of Sunni fundamentalist Islam. Still, the movement remained outside the political mainstream in the period of European domination and well into the period of independence, where the secular nationalist and leftist ideologies overshadowed it. The situation began to change as the political and economic retreat, which had begun in 1967 and was briefly interrupted in the 1970s, took a decisive turn to the worse beginning in the mid-1980s.

We should recall at this point that just as the liberal and nationalist doctrines may be said to correspond in their rise and elaboration to the growth—toward the end of the Ottoman and during the interwar periods—of a small urban bourgeoisie and educated elite, so the doctrine of socialism and mass revolution may be said to reflect, in its development and articulation following the Second World War, the emergence of a nascent urban proletariat and working class. But under the conditions of dependency and colonial occupation, neither the bourgeoisie nor the working class could develop into full-fledged social classes capable of gaining political control and determining the direction of social change. Thus, it was given to the in-between strata, the petty bourgeoisie and its smaller extensions, to emerge as the largest and most influential class that neopatriarchal society has thus far produced. Its rise made possible for the first time the formation of a *mass* movement. Until then all political movements had been essentially elitist or sectional and largely cut off from the grassroots of society; at no time had the nationalist or leftist parties been able to penetrate the proletarian mass and gain a truly mass following. Petty bourgeois fundamentalism was the first political ideology able to do this in a hundred years of neopatriarchy.[25]

The Ideological Factor

Let us now look at the content of this mass (counter)revolutionary movement. The petty bourgeois version of Islamic fundamentalism, though based on religious doctrine and inspired by religious principles, is not, properly speaking, a religious movement, at least not of the same order as the classical Islamic movements, such as the Wahhabi, the Sannusi, or the Mahdiyyah movements. Abstracted from its social and class context, fundamentalism could easily be read as the same sort of traditionalist Islamic ideology.[26] In its petty bourgeois form, however, fundamentalism can be properly understood only as a *political* phenomenon, the product of a specific historical, social, and economic moment. Thus, to give another parallel, a clear distinction should be made between the spontaneous religious impulse (or consciousness) of the Algerian or Sudanese peasant fighting against French or

British imperialism in the name of Islam, and the consciousness of a high school or college graduate Muslim Brother calling for the abolition of existing society and the building of
a new one. Fundamentalism in this latter form represents a
radical political ideology. It expresses the nostalgia of the
disinherited petty bourgeoisie for a lost golden age: an age of
faith, power, and justice, the absolute negation of the corrupt
and impotent established order. It represents the aspirations
of a social class that has failed to change society or itself and
now confronts external and internal threats which it cannot
overcome. Raising the slogan of Islamic struggle—for the
purification of society and the reinstatement of the true
faith—it seeks a way out of a situation that has become totally
intolerable.

A distinctive attitude of petty bourgeois fundamentalism is
its uncompromising opposition not only to secular nationalism but also to both Islamic reformism and establishment
conservatism, both of which it considers lacking in political
legitimacy—which explains its denunciation of *all* existing neopatriarchal regimes. Thus fundamentalism's triumph would
necessarily mean the dissolution of neopatriarchal society in
all its forms, for it seeks not only to destroy the structures of
the existing corrupt regimes, but also to replace them with
the one just (Islamic) society.

Still, petty bourgeois fundamentalism does not reject everything modern; it does not altogether repudiate what it calls
"modern civilization," which it defines in neutral terms. In
this sense it acknowledges the need for a particular kind of
modernity: for modern science and technology. It takes seriously the slogan Science and Faith—which is also manipulated, for their own purposes, by the conservative regimes—
and seeks to achieve an appropriate reconciliation between
the two practices. Viewed strictly pragmatically, the relation
of science to faith is limited to its instrumental value; so
while science as instrument and technology is recognized as
indispensable, as an *analytical* perspective (as theory and

method), it is relegated to a minor, rhetorical role. Truth and the conditions of its validation are determined by the word of God. In the end, as Sayyid Qutb, one of the leading intellectuals of militant fundamentalism and one of its great martyrs,[27] put it, "the question which Islam puts forth and to which it gives the answer is, Who is more knowledgeable, you or God?"[28] From this position, science is only a product or a means—and a dangerous double-edged sword.

On the psychological level, this fundamentalist vision provides an emotional shelter that neither scientific doctrine nor nationalist or socialist theory makes available. Paradoxically, while it promises apocalyptic change, it provides for reconciliation and coexistence with the status quo: it provides simultaneously for both obedience and revolt. This readiness equally to accept what is and to repudiate it sums up the contradictory impulses at the heart of neopatriarchal bourgeois fundamentalism. Whether this doctrine is used to instigate rebellion or to promote acquiescence, it is in both cases able to mobilize the masses on a scale hitherto unknown in neopatriarchal society. Here lies fundamentalism's central role in determining the course of the coming phase of Arab history.

The Fundamentalist Promise

The direction petty bourgeois fundamentalism is likely to take depends largely on how it resolves its internal ambivalence between rebellion and submission. A main obstacle to a clear resolution is practical, and may be formulated as follows: while fundamentalism as a social movement is an objective expression of class struggle, as a political consciousness it rejects the idea of class and class struggle (as did petty bourgeois nationalism), and in its political practice also rejects the tactics of the national front, the alliance of diverse forces and classes essential to confronting state power. In insisting, on the contrary, on classifying the members of society in terms of their "spiritual" being (religious relations) rather than their social being (social relations), it reduces the categories of both class and nation to those of religious community or religious brotherhood.

Revolt or submission? The ambivalence is deepened on the ideological level by the defection to fundamentalism, in the 1970s and 1980s, of a number of former Arab nationalist and Marxist intellectuals, seeking in it the substitute revolution. Precisely this kind of disillusionment gives fundamentalism its current petty bourgeois "revolutionism," rendering it an attractive alternative for failed secular activists who had so vehemently opposed religious ideology in the past. By the end of the 1970s, when secular ideology had reached its end and become politically impotent or irrelevant, only two choices remained besides secular modernism: cynicism (withdrawal) or fundamentalism (leap of faith).

But if fundamentalism now appeared to the educated and politically conscious as a kind of refuge, to the broad masses it constituted an only hope—the only remaining source of a sense of identity and power. The impoverished and illiterate masses intuitively grasped what fundamentalism proclaimed, for it stemmed directly from the monological, oral culture in which their consciousness was formed. The simple and direct articulation of fundamentalism presented the common person and the frustrated intellectual alike with a deeply satisfying world-view, one in which the self and the world were given in such comprehensiveness and consistency as to leave no question or doubt unanswered: Islamic fundamentalism promises immediate solutions to all the problems neither the secularist movements nor the existing regimes have been able to solve. From this vantage point all difficulties that loomed large now seemed surmountable, and ultimate victory inevitable.

What does this vision presuppose, and what does it foresee in concrete social terms? First of all, the complete transformation of existing (corrupt) society—from its present condition of "ignorance" (*jahiliyyah*) to a state of purity patterned after that of the Islamic *Jama'ah* (community)—is seen as a fairly simple task requiring only an act of faith or will: to reject the current *jahiliyyah* (neopatriarchal reality) and accept true Islam—in short, to be born again.[29] In times of crisis such conversions are easy and seem to generate their own validation. The new society is born immediately into the lives of the converted; it gets expressed overnight in their new life style, dress, appearance (beards), mode of discourse, daily prayer, and so forth.[30] Instantly, life is relieved of its burdens; the future becomes tolerable; daily existence is full of confidence and hope. This, however, is achieved not by dealing directly with the world and its problems, but by altering the terms of seeing these—that is, by changing the language (discourse) in which the social and historical problematic is interpreted. Thus, the question of modernity and traditionalism is resolved not through genuine resolution of the problem *in its own terms* (as the radical critics insist should be done), but by refusing to confront the problem directly and by explaining it away. Sayyid Qutb puts it this way: There are only two kinds of society, "an Islamic society and an Ignorant society (*jahiliyyah*)," and the good society is to be judged not according to humanity's needs or dreams but according to God's will.[31] "The greatest bondage," Qutb adds, "is subservience to human laws legislated by men."[32] The problem, then, is not one of choosing or finding a synthesis between two different kinds of societies but of submitting to the will of God and following the Prophet's example—an exegetical problem whose solution presents the various possible roads to utopia. As to who would be entrusted with providing the correct interpretation of God's will and with explaining the Prophet's words, it is assumed that the experts (i.e., the *ulema*) will. It can be seen how the epistemological problem concerning the nature of truth and validity—confronted by the secularist intellectuals in the early phase of the Awakening and taken up again nearly a century later by the modernist critics—is now again emptied of content and meaning by a sleight of hand: "The question which Islam poses and answers is this: Are you more knowledgeable

than God?"[33] If only the *right* questions are raised, then all
the correct answers will be made available. The displacement
of the possibility of critical analysis by theological exegesis
thus determines the terms of inquiry, and assures the outcome
of the right answers in advance.[34]

The feeling of dependency (inferiority) is approached from
the same transcendental standpoint and is overcome by a double "spiritual" movement: redefinition of the Self and the
alien Other. Consider the example provided by a book published in 1983 in Cairo under the title *Islam and the West*,
whose author makes the following assertion: "Muslims in their
religion and their institutions are the highest ideal of man on
earth in everything."[35] It would be wrong to construe this
statement in chauvinistic or ethnocentric terms. Its intent is
precisely to define the Self and the Other in the hyperbolic
naive terms made available by the current fundamentalist discourse. It is precisely in such terms that collective and individual frustrations are disposed of. Just by changing the terms
of reference, failure and its effects disappear. Thus, national
humiliation is overcome by simply eliminating the concept of
nationality and replacing it by that of religion (Islam, not the
[Arab] nation, is the ground of identity and selfhood, etc.).
Thus nationalism, in the view of the Syrian Da'wa fundamentalists (*al-Da'wa al-Islamiyyah*), is reduced to mere *'assabiyyah
jahiliyyah,* pre-Islamic ignorance.[36] From this view, the Muslim homeland is not the Arab world: "every land in which
Muslims live . . . is our homeland."[37] Qutb goes even further. "The homeland of the Muslim . . . is not just territory."[38] So it does not matter if the Arab nation is divided
and exploited, that the Arab nationalist movement is in sham-
bles. Failure, weakness, division, all ills are dismissed as mere
symptoms caused by abandoning Islam, by believing in the
false gods of nationalism, secularism, socialism, liberalism. Islam is the message of salvation of not only Arabs but all the
peoples of the world. The goal is global liberation. "The final
goal of our revolution is to establish Islam's peace on earth,

by the radical transformation of humanity as it exists to-day."[39]

The City of Allah

It is easy to see how from this messianic vision the waste of national resources, loss of Arab territory, defeat in war, and so forth, are treated as minor or insignificant setbacks.

In seeking to displace the "blasphemous" secular ideologies, political fundamentalism seeks to rewrite history and imprint on it its own vision of the past and future. This vision may be glimpsed in some detail from a rare and revealing document, a letter written in 1944 by the founder of the Muslim Brothers, Hassan al-Banna, and addressed to King Farouk and other Arab leaders and heads of states, in which he sets forth the fundamentalist view of what the Islamic society and state would look like in concrete terms. The letter is significant not only for the openness and clarity with which he describes the goals of radical fundamentalism, but for the specific details of his future Muslim society.

Banna's starting point is the crucial choice to be made, in the aftermath of the Second World War, between two possible roads, the "road of Islam—its sources, principles, learning, and civilization," and "the road of the West—its way of life, organization, and methods."[40]

Banna bases his choice not only on the intrinsic superiority of Islam but also on the fact that the West is bankrupt, defeated, and in a state of disintegration.[41] In the past, he points out,

the leadership of the world was "Eastern." But after the rise of Greece and Rome it became Western. Then after the rise of the prophetic religions, the Mosaic, the Christian and the Muhammadan, it became Eastern again. After that the East fell into deep sleep while the West arose in its modern renaissance. This is God's law which never changes; so the West seized world leadership, and it is still ruling and oppressing the world. . . . The time has come for a strong Eastern arm to raise the banner of God and the Quran (and to seize the leadership). The world will become Muslim and happy, and all the world will cry out: "Thanks be to the Almighty for guiding us, for without His guidance we could never have found the true path."[42]

Possessed of genuine Islam, the nation (and the world) will be imbued with the "organization, principles, emotions, and feelings" bestowed by the Quran. Banna describes, under the following heads, the Islamic precepts that would affect the different aspects of life:

1. "Islam and hope"
2. "Islam and military power"
3. "Islam and public health"
4. "Islam and science"
5. "Islam and ethics"
6. "Islam and economics"
7. "General Islamic organizations ('relating Islam to the individual, the family, the nation, the government, the people, and international relations.')"[43]

Banna then returns to the Western model and argues that the West could not serve as a guide to Muslims because the "Western experience" is different from theirs. To maintain that the West could provide the proper example for an "Eastern renaissance" is to misread history.

> Among the reasons why some Eastern countries have left the [road of] Islam in favor of the Western way is the conviction of some of their leaders that the Western renaissance was achieved by destroying religion, by pulling down the churches and getting rid of papal authority and the power of the clergy . . . and by separating church from state. But if these measures proved effective in the Western nations they cannot work in Islam because the nature of our religion and its teachings are different from those of any other religion; however, the power of the Muslim clergy is too limited to change the existing structures or to overturn the established regimes. Because Islamic principles have not changed across the centuries, they are for this very reason suitable for every age; these

principles stand for progress, science, and the protection of the men of science.[44]

And he adds:

> Your Majesty: In light of this we have no excuse for failing to take the road of truth, the Islamic road, and for taking instead the path of desire and decoration, the European road.
>
> So be the first to go forward in the name of the Prophet, bearing the medicine of the Quran to save this sick and suffering world.[45]

Then he turns to the main issue, the question of "practical reforms," which he deals with in three sections, one on "political, legal, and administrative matters," another on "social and scientific aspects," and a third on "economics."

In the first section he calls for "reforming the law so that it would conform with the Islamic *Shari'a*"; for "serious and practical" effort to restore the office of the caliphate; for regulation of governmental organizations and activities so that "celebrations, official meetings and conventions, prisons, and hospitals would not contradict Muslim prescriptions and work would not conflict with prayer"; for "monitoring the personal conduct of [government] employees"; and for "placing al-Azhar graduates in military and administrative posts and providing them with the appropriate training."[46]

In the second section, on "social and scientific matters," he first underscores the need to teach people to "respect public morals" by following "directives reinforced by law [and] by stiffening punishment of moral crimes." He then addresses the question of women and calls for a "cure," which would, as he puts it, "elevate" the woman as well as "protect" her, so that this question, "which is one of the most important in society," would not be left to the whims and "wild ideas" of "ideological" writers. And he suggests the following practical measures: eradicating prostitution—"both legal and illegal," and punishing violators by public whipping; prohibiting alcohol and fighting it "as one would fight drugs"; proscribing makeup and all forms of exhibitionism, and "instructing women in what is proper," that is, proper dress and behavior, "particularly women teachers, women students, and women doctors"; revising school curricula, with separate ones for girls and boys; forbidding coeducation in schools and making it a crime for a man and a woman (unless married) to meet or be alone together; introducing religious education in schools and universities; closing down nightclubs, prohibiting dancing; "monitoring theaters and movies" and censoring "plays, films, books, newspapers, and radio programs"; and designing a uniform "for the nation as a whole."[47]

The final section (on economics) proposes the following reforms: making payment of *zakat* (tithe) systematic and regular, so as to support "such necessary charitable projects as homes for the elderly, poor, and orphans, and for strengthening the army"; prohibiting interest; encouraging "economic projects . . . and providing work for the unemployed"; protecting the public from "greedy and monopolistic companies"; raising the salaries of the small employees and reducing the salaries of the big bureaucrats; "encouraging agricultural education"; "giving special attention to the professional work and social conditions of workers"; and "utilizing [unused] natural resources, such as unused land and abandoned mines and so on."[48]

Thus fundamentalism, as advocated by Banna and his disciples, presents itself as the alternative to capitalism and socialism and the only valid doctrine for Muslim society. In fundamentalism, now its dominant ideology, neopatriarchal society provides the condition of its own dissolution. Just as the triumph of secularism (in nationalist or socialist forms) would have led to the disappearance of neopatriarchy (by transforming it into modernity), fundamentalism now promises to undermine neopatriarchal society by the opposite transformation—return to patriarchy.

How would fundamentalism accomplish this? If a fundamentalist upheaval or revolution on the Iranian model is unlikely—because of the absence of a unified leadership, the cooptive or coercive power of the state apparatus, and so forth—what kind of upheaval is Arab Islamic fundamentalism capable of triggering?

Militant petty bourgeois fundamentalism is already the dominant ideological force within Arab neopatriarchal society, and constitutes the greatest *potential* (counter)revolutionary force within it. We can already see its radically destabilizing impact in the transformation of consciousness taking place among vast lower strata of the population. It seems possible that traditional patriarchy in its fundamentalist petty bourgeois form could prevail in the near future, if not through revolution or generalized violence then just through the erosion of neopatriarchy's ideological legitimacy and political forms.

There is now a good chance for the struggle which was first joined at the beginning of the age of Awakening—between the New and the Old, between secular modernity and traditional patriarchy—now to be settled, in its final phase, by the triumph of the Old, of patriarchy dressed in petty bourgeois fundamentalism. But it is just as likely that the struggle may take a new and purer form, one in which radical secular criticism would rise to challenge radical fundamentalism. That the former might at this juncture appear at a serious disadvantage is due more to external conditions than internal weakness—to the fact that frightened ruling classes find it easier to suppress modernist criticism calling for the reexamination of what is, than to oppose militant fundamentalism brandishing the sacred scriptures and invoking God's wrath.

Precisely because the status quo might for some time be able to contain the *political* onslaught of militant fundamentalism (rather than its ideological and social advance), the first battle might be waged—at least in the initial stages—in the cultural and intellectual arena, pitting against each other the two forces whose goal is to uproot and to replace the existing neopatriarchal order.

10

What Is To Be Done?

It is true, liberation can never be a fix. This is the hard lesson the last Arab generation has, over the past thirty years, learned and suffered.

Fundamentalists now invoke the same cataclysmic vision of redemption as did the defeated secular nationalist and leftist ideologists. Earlier I held out the hope that a fundamentalist revolution might, by bringing down the structure of neopatriarchy, contribute to radical change. Such a possibility can have no basis in reality. For even if fundamentalism were to gain the upper hand in some Arab country or countries, what guarantee is there that it would bring about *any basic* change in the existing neopatriarchal structure? The likelihood rather is that with a fundamentalist victory, the essence of neopatriarchal society would survive.

What would be the outcome were Fundamentalism to gain power on a regional scale? A report put out by the Swedish Defense Research Institute in 1985 takes this possibility seriously.

Seen in a longer perspective most of the nations of today's Middle East are artificial creations which were the work of Britain and France in 1919 and 1920. After the colonial powers were forced to leave the area at the end of the Second World War, the system of states which they bequeathed has also gradually crumbled away. Since 1947 Palestine has been the scene of repeated warfare, Cyprus has been split in two since 1974, Lebanon has been mangled and

fragmented chiefly by civil strife since 1975, while Iran and Iraq
have been engaged in war since 1980. If these trends should continue there are manifest risks of Syria and Iraq for instance (both
heterogeneous political units like Lebanon) facing collapse if and
when the present dictatorships disappear. The small Gulf Sheik-
doms are also political formations of recent date, and all of them
live with neighbouring countries harboring territorial claims. This
scenario of anarchy, fraught with unpredictable risks of sabotage
aimed at the oil plants and of uncontrollable outbreaks of war,
represents a very unpleasant yet hardly unthinkable possibility for
the future.[1]

A successful Islamic fundamentalist revolution, carried to
its logical conclusion (e.g., as it was in Iran), would probably
fulfill the conditions necessary for temporarily ending direct
dependency on the West and for waging sustained war against
imperialism and settler colonialism. Neither the prospect nor
the modality of such revolution, however, can be foreseen.

The other hypothetical and equally transformative revolution comes from the opposite direction: a socialist revolution
on the Maoist model—as suggested by Samir Amin in 1976.
Only such a revolution would be able, by

its renunciation of Western patterns of consumption and, to some
extent, of Western technologies . . . to transcend them. This dis-
engagement operates as a powerful force of liberation, allowing the
people to understand in practical terms that neither these patterns
of consumption nor these technologies are neutral. It makes it possible to affirm relations of production which, in their denial of these
Western patterns, favor a development of the productive forces
capable of overtaking that which capitalism has achieved.[2]

How can this come about?

Firstly, a broad anti-imperialist front must be constituted. Secondly,
the leadership of this front must be assessed by an ideologically and
organizationally autonomous working class, in close alliance with
the impoverished peasantry.[3]

Some ten years later, when fundamentalism had become
ascendant and the left overwhelmed, Amin reconsidered his
earlier judgment. A socialist revolution was now impossible,
for the class historically designated to carry it out lacks the

ideology and the organization to do so.[4] Hence the unpredictability of the future.

It is impossible on our modernity-patriarchy model to construct a scenario of the future, much less talk about revolutionary modalities. The applicability of our model stops at the point where neopatriarchal society breaks down (or is brought down), and where, within the cleared social space, the inauguration of modernity becomes an objective possibility.

From this view, "liberation" no longer appears as a cataclysmic "all at once," but rather the product of an extended process of transformation and change occurring in three basic areas: in the material infrastructure (e.g., rational economic development); within social institutions (e.g., the progressive nuclearization of the family); and in political practice (as we shall discuss).

In this respect, liberation need no longer be linked to the classical revolutionary *seizure* of power. One of the great insights of structuralist analysis is in showing that power is not only present in its visible and traditional forms but is immanent and pervasive, inhabiting complex networks devoid of subjectivity and broadly diffused in discursive and social practices. To overthrow a despotic or reactionary regime will not guarantee freedom and justice. From this perspective, one of the conditions of liberation is the destruction of the old neopatriarchal conception of liberation.

What our model of modernity and patriarchy *can* provide is an elucidation of the conditions under which the liberation project can be pursued in the period of transition. Thus, while our model would agree that neopatriarchy is not likely to be transcended by "education" or "modernization" or "development," it rejects the possibility of "all at once" solutions. It takes note of the inexorable movement of history; from this standpoint, China, Algeria, and Vietnam all belong to a different world, as do the revolutionary theories and interpretations based on them. Revolutionary thought can become retrograde and be absorbed into the neopatriarchal "regime of truth." Criticism is not a luxury but rather a matter of vital need, not just for instituting a "careful and critical discourse" that can yield fresh, self-critical consciousness, but also for deconstructing and transcending the prevailing neopatriarchal consciousness that has bounded and immobilized thought and practice for over a century. An effective critique then presents itself as a first requirement in the process of subverting the neopatriarchal discourse and clearing the way for the possibility of modernity.

What should be the immediate goal of such an effort?

The first goal should be the devising of new and realistic modes of theorizing. Consider the futility of the progressive or revolutionary models of neopatriarchal ideology: the bourgeois model of parliamentary democracy—an antiquated political order that has no basis in Third World social reality and experience; the nationalist model of complete pan-Arab unity—perhaps a realistic and feasible goal until the creation of the twenty-two entrenched sovereignties, and now a quixotic dream; the revolutionary vision (Marxist or Maoist) which ignores the state of the world and the region's barely reformist situation (1917 is nowhere in sight and 1905 is but a distant mirage!). In this context it is not surprising that the goal of democracy should appear almost utopian—let alone that of implementing unity or carrying out the revolution. In other words, concepts of political democracy, unity, social justice, and so forth, must be rethought in the light of past experience and refashioned in terms of existing new reality.

At stake at this juncture is not the fate of any particular ideology or regime, but society's very survival—a proclamation which neopatriarchal rhetoric mystifies by constantly reiterating. The threat comes not only from external sources—settler colonialism, and imperialism—but also from internal social disintegration and economic collapse, from inter-Arab conflict and civil war. Only a force from within Arab society will be able to hold it together. Waiting for the revolution to change the status quo is not a revolutionary stance. Truly radical action will undertake the difficult task of addressing feasible possibilities: possibilities to be found in the structures and institutions of the status quo, not in a utopian vision.

Can we change the relation between the state and its citizens from one based on violence to one based on law? Perhaps, but only by legal methods and by means based on public consent. The seizure of power, experience has shown, will not guarantee this. Violence will always lurk in the background and can be legitimately invoked (certainly where settler colonialism persists); but commitment to legal, nonviolent terms of political exchange may, at least in certain regimes, lead to some concrete results: limiting violence, humanizing social relations, liberalizing political life. In concrete terms, the most immediate concern right now might be the question of human and political rights. Why should the attainment of these rights appear such a remote possibility? The new generation, which has known only repression and violence, will find in this objective a truly revolutionary task—if only it can grasp the radical significance of retrieving these rights, and the long-term consequences of such a possibility for the existing political arrangement.

I can feel the scorn of the neopatriarchal "revolutionary" reader contemplating these reformist—indeed, seemingly counterrevolutionary—remarks. But the inadequacy of neopatriarchal revolutionism must sooner or later become obvious—its failure to achieve its goals, its blindness to history, and its retreat to ineffective sloganeering. Why should it be impossible to throw the status quo—for years equipped and ready to deal swiftly with violent opposition but not with nonviolent protest—off balance, by facing it with an approach based on demands of civil and political rights and democratic legality?

Again, these are the questions to which I am seeking some answers: What does it take to shift the existing order's enforcement of stability from violence to law? What is necessary to compel the state to speak the language of law rather than the language of force? What is needed to make power take its own laws seriously? Why should the transition from the *machstaat* to the *rechtstaat* appear such an impossible undertaking?

Once more, this is not to say that the coming phase will necessarily be spared violence or the need to resort to it. I am merely saying that for the immediate future there are other, nonviolent and effective measures that could be pursued. Just as the conditions of struggle change, so do its means. Could it be that violence, precisely perhaps because it has become so pervasive, has lost its effectiveness? Strictly and in pragmatic terms violence, at least for the time being, has become self-defeating. Choosing to wage the struggle for basic human rights—in relation to which all other struggles are ultimately derivative—could be a decisive choice, not only for safeguarding the integrity of Arab society, but also for eventually achieving liberation and justice. In the internal struggle for freedom and democracy, armed struggle may at certain moments appear antiquated and carnivalesque, and taking the risk of nonviolence and civil disobedience the true heroism.

Periods of transition, Lukacs wrote, are times of crisis but also renewal. "Every great historical period is a period of transition, a contradictory unity of . . . destruction and rebirth; a new social order and a new type of man always comes into being in the course of a unified though contradictory process."[5]

The way to renewal, in terms of the radical-democratic paradigm I have been trying to elucidate, requires a method that is both *critical* and *contestatory:* critical in the manner of the different disciplines and approaches of the radical critics (without, however, any of them enjoying a hegemonic or privileged position); and contestatory in a dialogical, nonviolent way, with civil disobedience as its basic form of struggle.

Such practice would involve various forms of organizing: single individuals (intellectuals), groups of individuals organized in professional workers', women's, and students' organizations, as well as political parties and groups; it would be predicated on pluralist representation, with professors, writers, artists, doctors, lawyers, clergymen, workers, students, and women joining together in common struggle. The terrain of such practice lies obviously within individual countries; the possibilities and the nature of struggle would differ from country to country—some regimes being open to change, others closed; it is in closed countries that violence may ultimately prove inescapable.

The objectives of struggle can no longer be sectional, sectarian, or ideologically restricted, but must be *universal* and widely acknowledged—acknowledged by the majority as right and correct and politically feasible.

The *general* and most basic objectives are those implied by *human* and *political* rights: the human rights acknowledged by the Declaration of Human Rights (and as in the specific interpretation of the Arab Organization for Human Rights); and the political rights laid down in the constitutions and legal provisions of the different Arab countries, including the rights of political participation, election of representatives, and formation of political parties.

Specific objectives focus on the formation of national and pan-Arab vehicles for social and political action: professional associations (academic, medical, legal), trade unions, peasant cooperatives, students' and women's organizations, and autonomous organizations of every kind.

Of all these groups, potentially the most revolutionary is the women's movement. If this phase of struggle were to open up to radical democratic change, women's liberation would necessarily be its spearhead. Even in the short term, the women's movement is the detonator which will explode neopatriarchal society from within. If allowed to grow and come into its own, it will become the permanent shield against patriarchal regression, the cornerstone of future modernity.

Let me stress again, the above considerations outline the

conditions of possibility for radical democratic change; they do not constitute an agenda or program for action. Such a program or agenda can only be put together by men and women living and working under concrete conditions, driven to act collectively.

As some of us know, the Arab world (Arab society) is, for the most part, a culturally and politically desolate and oppressive place in which to live and to work. It is a difficult place in which to struggle to build a decent and humane society—and for the liberation of women, without the achievement of "conscious" intellectuals, the future may hold much less than my remarks might lead one to hope for. It is perhaps my wishful impulse to overcome the paralyzing cultural trauma that has dominated my generation and might now take hold of the younger one, which impels me to affirm society's ability not only to survive but also to overcome its innermost disease, neopatriarchy, and to become modern.

I must, then, proclaim not only the inevitable victory of the rising radical democratic forces over both the neopatriarchal status quo and its fundamentalist destroyers-redeemers, but also the coming of modernity, secular democracy, and libertarian socialism. Yes. To fight the pessimism of the intellect, one must hold fast to the optimism of the will.

Notes

Chapter 1

1. Ali Zay'our, *The Psychoanalysis of the Arab Self* (Beirut, 1977), p. 122 (Arabic).
2. Here I refer to the relation of dependency theorized particularly in A. G. Frank, *Capitalism and Underdevelopment* (New York, 1967) and Samir Amin, *Unequal Development: Social Formations at the Periphery of the Capitalist System* (New York, 1976).
3. *al-Ahram,* May 17, 1977. Quoted in John J. Donohue and John L. Esposito, eds., *Islam in Transition: Muslim Perspectives* (New York, 1982), p. 240.
4. See Samih K. Farsoun, "State Capitalism and Counter-Revolution in the Middle East: A Thesis," in B. Kaplan, ed., *Social Change in the Capitalist World Economy* (Beverly Hills, 1978), pp. 139–56.
5. Such a reading, according to Muhammad Arkoun, would incorporate the critical approaches of modern linguistics, anthropology, psychoanalysis, structuralism, and Marxism. "Rethinking Islam" (Lecture at Georgetown University, October 30, 1985).

Chapter 2

1. Fernand Braudel, *Capitalism and Material Life, 1400–1800,* trans. Miriam Kochan (New York, 1973), p. 31. According to Braudel the lack of plentiful wood in the Arab world and its

abundance in Europe was a major factor in the decline of the former and the strong growth of the latter.

2. *Grundrisse,* trans. Martin Nicolaus (London, 1973), pp. 483–89. This is not the place to address the problem of Marx's Eurocentric bias, which has been the subject of recent debate; see, for example, Umberto Melotti, *Marx and the Third World,* trans. Pat Ransford (London, 1977), pp. 70–76.

3. For the most part, with the exception of Egypt.

4. Marshall Berman, *All That Is Solid Melts into Air* (New York, 1982), pp. 15–36, 106–112.

5. The full account of this phenomenon has been given in Fernand Braudel, *Civilsation materielle, économie et capitalisme: XV–XVIIIe siècle,* (Paris, 1979). Trans. Sian Reynolds: *Civilization and Capitalism: The Wheels of Commerce,* vol. 2 (New York, 1982).

6. Berman, *All That Is Solid,* p. 106.

7. Ibid., p. 109.

8. Ibid., p. 109.

9. Ibid., p. 112.

10. *Communist Manifesto* (Arlington Heights, ILL: Harlan Davidson, 1955), p. 13.

11. In neopatriarchal society, stripping away the veil is the sign of rebellion *and* modernity.

12. Following Berman's approach. *All That Is Solid,* pp. 569–71.

13. "To be modern is to find ourselves in an environment that promises us adventure, power, joy, growth, transformation of ourselves and the world—and, at the same time, that threatens to destroy everything we have, everything we know, everything we are." Ibid., p. 15.

14. This is a convenient place to make the comparison with Japan. In Japan the tension between modernization and tradition took a radically different form from that in Arab Muslim society. Whereas in the Arab world Westernizers and traditionalists were polarized and engaged socially in open ideological (and later political) struggle, in Japan the conflict remained inside the individual; the Japanese people as a whole maintained adherence to official ideology. Thus the problem in Arab society remained an open *social* and *politi-*

cal problem without social or political resolution. In Japan it was successfully resolved on the political level but remained problematic on the social level. See Thomas C. Smith, *The Agrarian Origins of Modern Japan* (Stanford, 1959), p. 206.

15. "To be a Levantine is to live in two worlds or more at once, without belonging to either; to be able to go through the external forms which indicate the possession of a certain nationality, religion or culture, without actually possessing it. It is no longer to have a standard of values of one's own, not to be able to create but only able to imitate; and so not even to imitate correctly, since that also needs a certain originality. It is to belong to no community and to possess nothing of one's own. It reveals itself in lostness, pretentiousness, cynicism and despair." A. H. Hourani, *Syria and Lebanon* (London, 1946), pp. 70–71.

16. Including technocrats, professionals, educators, writers, and creative artists.

17. The best example of this can be seen in the poetry journal *Shi'r (Poetry)* (Beirut, 1957–1963) and the movement centered around it. The movement flourished in the 1950s and 1960s and introduced in Arabic translation T. S. Eliot, Ezra Pound, Saint John Perse, Eric Maria Rilke, and René Char, among others.

Chapter 3

1. Neopatriarchy simultaneously involves the disintegration of patriarchal relations and the emergence of modern relations. The contradictions inherent in neopatriarchy are similar to those present in capitalism, with both systems forming a final phase in a historical continuum.

2. It is worth noting that the mode of production characteristic of precapitalist forms of Arab Muslim patriarchy was never based on chattel slavery (as was the Greco-Roman formation) or on feudal serfdom (as was medieval Europe), a fact which gave the Arab Muslim patriarchy its peculiar character. A good deal of research is needed to provide a clearer picture of the various premodern stages or types of patriarchy, especially

with regard to the system of ownership and the division of labor which prevailed until the late eighteenth and early nineteenth centuries.

3. W. Montgomery Watt, *Muhammad at Medina* (Oxford, 1956), pp. 327–28.

4. "Basic" in the sense used by Maslow: see section below entitled "Patriarchy and Nationalistic Consciousness" and note 17.

5. *Grundrisse,* trans. Martin Nicolaus (London, 1973), p. 472.

6. See my *Introduction to the Study of Arab Society* (Beirut, 1980), pp. 27–47 (in Arabic). Here I take it as given that adult behavior reflects the dominant cultural modalities of socialization. From the perspective of psychoanalysis, certain characteristics of Arab culture—modes of adult political and social behavior—become understandable in the light of child-rearing and socialization practices.

7. *Grundrisse,* p. 472.

8. *al-Mar'a wal-Jins,* 2nd ed. (Cairo, 1972).

9. *Beyond the Veil: Male-Female Dynamics in a Modern Muslim Society* (Cambridge, MA, 1975).

10. The first important reformist writer is Qasim Amin, author of *al-Mar'a al-Jadidah (Modern Woman)* (Cairo, 1899) and *Tahrir al-Mar'a (The Liberation of Woman)* (Cairo, 1900). The conservative position was expressed by the mainstream Muslim clergy, led by the al-Azhar *'ulema.*

11. Sadawi, *Women and Sexuality,* pp. 18–19.

12. Mernissi, *Beyond the Veil,* p. viii.

13. Sadawi, *Women and Sexuality,* pp. 167–68.

14. Ibid., p. 168.

15. George Tarabishi, *Women and Socialism* (Beirut, n.d.) (Arabic). Quoted in Mernissi, *Beyond the Veil,* p. 103.

16. Mernissi, *Beyond the Veil,* pp. 103, 107.

17. These three needs coincide with Maslow's hierarchy of "basic" needs, in which "physiological," "safety," and "belongingness and love" needs are regarded as foremost in the structure of human motivation. See A. H. Maslow, *Motivation and Personality* (New York, 1954), pp. 80–98.

18. In one's struggle for survival, one can only rely on the protection and help of those nearest one, with whom one identifies

and to whom one belongs—one's family, kin, and coreligionists. As we shall see, loyalty and solidarity are relations grounded in these primary structures, rather than in the political structure of the (modern) state.

19. Carolyn Lee Baum and Richard Baum, "Creating the New Communist Child: Continuity and Change in Chinese Styles of Early Childhood Socialization," in K. Wilson, A. A. Wilson, and S. L. Greenblatt, eds., *Value Change in Chinese Society* (New York, 1979), p. 103.

Chapter 4

1. Interestingly, Freud defines the external social structure, the "external world" as that "in which the individual finds himself exposed after being detached from his parents." *An Outline of Psychology* (New York, 1970), pp. 123–24.
2. Ali Zay'our, *The Psychoanalysis of the Arab Self* (Beirut, 1977) (in Arabic).
3. Ibid., p. 5.
4. Ibid., p. 34.
5. For a living portrayal of the father as absolute patriarch, see the novel by Naguib Mahfouz, *Bayn al-Qasrayn (Between Two Palaces)* (Cairo, [1956]), pp. 6, 14, 19–20, 58, 140–141.
6. Zay'our, *Psychoanalysis of the Arab Self*, p. 34.
7. Ibid.
8. Ibid.
9. The converse of patriarchal dependence and oppression is the pathological "autonomy" produced by advanced capitalist relations. "The more profound the sense of social powerlessness the more luxurious the growth of 'personal' hyperbole. The other is simultaneously a means and an obstruction to my ends. Each of us simultaneously chooses and is compelled to be free, so that continuously more seclusive independence is constantly prescribed." Richard Lichtman, *Production of Desire: The Integration of Psychoanalysis and Marxist Theory* (New York, 1982), p. 225.
10. Zay'our, *Psychoanalysis of the Arab Self*, p. 160.
11. Recall that Reich's central theme, like Zay'our's, is that the individual's psychic structure corresponds to the existing so-

cial order. Thus Arab psychological structure is achieved through socialization in the neopatriarchal family.

12. Jean Piaget, *The Essential Piaget,* ed. Howard E. Guber and J. Jacques Vonèche (New York, 1977).

13. Ibid., p. 156.

14. Ibid., p. 150.

15. Ibid., pp. 157–58.

16. Ibid., pp. 178–79.

17. Piaget emphasizes "cooperation," the practical expression of mutual recognition and esteem, as the basis of autonomy, which is achieved by equality. "From the moment that it replaces the rule of constraint . . . the rule of cooperation becomes an effective moral law. . . . This can develop only through the progress made by cooperation and mutual respect—cooperation between children to begin with, and then between child and adult as the child approaches adolescence and comes, secretly at least, to consider himself as the adult's equal." Ibid., pp. 179, 190. Juergen Habermas discusses transition from heteronomy to autonomy in terms of transition from "role-identity" to "ego-identity," from "stagnation" (traditionality) to "activity" (modernity). "The transition from stagnation to activity, from role-identity to ego-identity, involves a radical transformation in the conditions of existence which is expressed in a transition from personal identity no longer constituted by the values and forms of inherited cultural tradition, but established by the possession of critical procedures [of thought]." See *Communication and the Evolution of Society,* trans. Thomas McCarthy (New York, 1970), p. 72.

18. Wilhelm Reich, *The Sexual Revolution: Toward a Self-Regulating Character Structure,* trans. Theodore P. Wolfe (New York, 1974), p. 72.

Chapter 5

1. *The Arab Nation* (London, 1978), pp. 21–23.

2. *Grundrisse* (London, 1978), p. 473.

3. Amin, *The Arab Nation,* p. 23.

4. Marc Bloch, *Feudal Society*, trans. L. A. Manyon (Chicago, 1974), vol. 2, p. 443.

5. Max Weber, whose grasp of Islamic history and society was strongly intuitive, was struck by the quality to which Amin alludes—the "warrior ethic" of Islam, a central category for Weber's interpretation of the Islamic ethos.

6. Bloch, *Feudal Society*, p. 452.

7. Montesquieu, with the Ottoman sultan in mind, adds, "[Where] the prince declares himself proprietor of all the lands, heir to all his subjects . . . nothing is repaired or improved. Houses are built only for the necessity of habitation; there is no digging of ditches or planting of trees; everything is drawn from, but nothing is restored to the earth; the ground lies untilled, and the whole country becomes desert." *The Spirit of the Laws* (New York, 1949), vol. 1, p. 65.

8. See William Hardy Wickwar, *The Modernization of Administration in the Near East* (Beirut, 1963), pp. 59–62.

9. In contrast, when Japan opened up to Europe a little over half a century later, it was economically, politically, and culturally prepared to deal with modernization on its own terms and without falling prey to Western domination.

10. These are covered by the *tanzimat* that began with the promulgation in 1839 of the *Hatti Sherif of Gulhane*. See J. C. Hurewitz, *The Middle East and North Africa: A Documentary Record* (New Haven, 1975), pp. 269–70 ff.

Chapter 6

1. Gleri Shirokov, "Colonies and Dependent Countries," *Social Science* [Moscow] (Summer, 1984), p. 160.

2. Ibid., p. 166.

3. Bassim Mussallam in a lecture given at Georgetown University, September 18, 1984. This thesis, at least where Egypt is concerned, is opposed by Samir Amin, who views the theory of a "renaissance" as a distortion of bourgeois intellectuals. "Only the colonial alienation of the modern epoch can explain why, even in Egyptian historiography, eighteenth-century Egypt is held to be 'feudal' and 'decadent' and there-

fore dependent on Europe to realize its 'renaissance,' " Samir
Amin, "Contradictions in the Capitalist Development of
Egypt: A Review Essay," *Monthly Review* (September, 1984),
pp. 15–18.

4. Frantz Fanon, *Dying Colonialism* (New York: 1965), p. 179.
See also Marx's reference, in *The German Ideology* (New
York, 1967), p. 69, to the "muck of the ages," the psychological distortion of which the oppressed must rid themselves to
achieve genuine emancipation.

5. Jean-Paul Sartre, introduction to *The Colonizer and the Colonized,* by Albert Memmi, trans. Howard Greenfield (New
York, 1965), p. xxvi.

6. Elizabeth Monroe, *Britain's Moment in the Middle East,
1914–1917* (Baltimore, 1981), p. 15.

7. Attempts were made to "improve" the status and lot of the
indigenous inhabitants by various means. The Algerians particularly were given the formal option of becoming French
citizens, but under certain conditions. For example, as the
Senatus Consultu of 1865 stipulated, one could do so if one
renounced one's status as a Muslim, or, after the First World
War under the 1919 electoral law, if one was monogamous,
had no record of crime or "hostility toward the French, [was]
able to speak or write the French language, had served in the
French army, and was a property owner.") The Libyans and
Palestinians were subjected to different kinds of treatment.
Many Libyans were pushed into reservations at the edge of
the desert (the bulk of them would have probably died except for the Second World War and the defeat of Fascist
Italy). The Palestinians, instantly made pariahs in their own
homeland with the establishment of the Jewish state in 1948,
were granted either citizenship—not as a national group with
national rights but as members of the "non-Jewish minorities"—or, in the occupied West Bank and Gaza, simply the
status of "residents" or "inhabitants;" or were made into
refugees.

8. Colonial relations created a dehumanizing view of the colonized, as almost belonging to a different category of being.
"All the terms used to describe the colonized—uncivilized, sav-
age, primitive, traditional—convey the categorical separation

of the colonizer and the colonized. The essence of colonialism in this literature is much more profound than military occupation. For true colonialism to take place—in contrast to the old-style political imperialism—the colonized must be transformed from an individual with belief in himself or herself as a capable human being to one who believes *only in the capacity of others*." (Italics added.) Martin Carnoy, *Education as Cultural Imperialism* (New York, 1974), pp. 26–27.

9. Edward Said, *Orientalism* (New York, 1978).

10. "With vision of a future radically different from the past," as Thomas C. Smith put it. *The Agrarian Origins of Modern Japan* (Stanford, 1959), p. 201.

11. For instance, one reason put forth for the disintegration of the Dhofar revolution in the 1970s, potentially one of the most explosive in the recent history of the Arabian peninsula, was the leadership's insistence on using Marxist rather than familiar religious terminology in addressing its followers and supporting population.

12. Fanon, who thought highly of the power of tradition in the struggle against colonialism, was also aware of the reactionary potential of traditional movements. "To bring abandoned tradition to life again does not only mean going against the current of history but also opposing one's own people." *The Wretched of the Earth*, trans. Constance Farrington (New York, 1963), p. 224.

13. Mustafa Khalidi and ʿUmar Farroukh, *al-Tabshir wʾal-Istiʿmar fil-Buldan al-ʿArabiyya (The Missionary Movements and Colonialism in the Arab Countries)*. (Beirut, 1953).

14. Ibid., p. 56.

15. Ibid., p. 17.

16. Ibid.

17. Carnoy, *Education as Cultural Imperialism*, p. 27, n. 4.

18. *The Lord* (London, 1985), p. 22.

19. "A Modern Missionary," *Atlantic Monthly* (May 1920), pp. 664–675. Reprinted in Stephen Penrose, Jr., *That They May Have Life* (New York, 1941), pp. 181–82.

20. Ibid.

21. Ibid.

22. "Statement by Dr. Bliss to the Versailles Peace Conference,

1919," Appendix K, in Penrose, *That They May Have Life,* pp. 328–29.

23. Inaugural address given at American University of Beirut, June 28, 1923), in Penrose, *That They May Have Life,* pp. 292–94.

24. Paulo Freire, *Pedagogy of the Oppressed,* trans. Myra Bergman Ramos (New York, 1970), p. 135.

25. Taha Hussein, *Memoirs* (Beirut, 1967), p. 11 (Arabic). Other important Egyptian writers of this period include Tawfiq al-Hakim, 'Abbas al-'Aqad, Mahmud Taimur, and Ibrahim al-Mazini.

26. Most active in the Arab world during the post-World War II period have been the Ford, Rockefeller, and Carnegie foundations.

27. See, for example, Robert F. Arnove, ed., *Philanthropy and Cultural Imperialism: The Foundations at Home and Abroad* Bloomington, IN, 1982).

28. Ibid., pp. 322–23.

29. E. Berman, "The Foundations' Role in American Foreign Policy: The Case of Africa, post 1945)," in ibid., p. 212.

Chapter 7

1. See Roland Barthes, *Elements of Semiology,* trans. Annette Lavers and Collin Smith (New York, 1968), p. 14.

2. Colin MacCabe, "On Discourse," *Economy and Society* (August 1979), p. 279.

3. Frederic Jameson, *The Political Unconscious* (Ithaca, NY, 1981), p. 297.

4. One exception is Israel; but Hebrew was intentionally introduced to provide a single language to replace the several languages of Jews emigrating to Israel from various countries, and to secure national unity by reverting to the traditional language. It should be noted, however, that Israeli Hebrew has been consciously transformed in its vocabulary and use into a modern language.

5. The implications of this have been carefully noted by Adonis (Ahmad 'Ali Sa'id), *The Permanent and the Changing, A*

Study in Imitation and Creativity, vol. 1 (Beirut, 1974–1978), p. 29 (Arabic).

6. Halim Barakat, *Contemporary Arab Society* (Beirut, 1984), p. 246 (in Arabic).

7. Adonis, *The Permanent and the Changing,* p. 29.

8. To use Roland Barthes' term. *The Pleasure of the Text,* trans. Richard Miller (New York, 1975), p. 40.

9. Jacques Berque, *Arab Rebirth: Pain and Ecstasy,* trans. Quentin Hoare (London, 1983), p. 27.

10. Ibid.

11. This, for example, is how the truth of the prophet's traditions (*hadith*), and that of Muslim historiography (*ta'rikh*) are constituted: their reality is the text, itself the reflection and repository of the oral narrative chain.

12. In the patriarchal setting, as Claude Levi-Strauss has shown, narrative fulfills a social and a psychological function, by verbally, "in the imaginary," reconciling socially irreconcilable contradictions; as such, narrative is an act through which the patriarchal individual seeks to resolve crucial problems. In the neopatriarchal setting, however, where the character of the real has been transformed, narrative becomes a form of escape or wishful thinking.

13. Quoted in Roland Barthes, "Inaugural Lecture, College de France," *A Barthes Reader,* ed. Susan Sontag (New York, 1982), p. 460.

14. Mustafa Lutfi al-Manfaluti, *al-Fadilah (Virtue)* (Beirut, 1969), Bernandin de Saint Pierre, *Paul et Virginie* (Paris, 1878).

15. In the case of Japan, the transfer was virtually completed in a generation and a half, between 1866 and 1900.

16. The general notion I have in mind here follows Michel Foucault's epistemic orders, Thomas Kuhn's theory of paradigms, and Louis Althusser's "epistemological rupture" in Marx.

17. The earliest and one of the best examples of the language and discourse of the *nahda* is provided by Faris al-Shidyaq in his remarkable book, *al-Saq 'ala-Saq,* a rambling autobiographical account first printed (in Arabic) in Paris in 1855 (Paris: Benjamin Dupart; reprinted, Beirut, Dar Maktabat al-Hayat, 1967), in some respects one of the most original works of the Awakening.

18. The political side of how this was accomplished has been fully narrated by George Antonius, *The Arab Awakening* (Philadelphia, 1938); the cultural and ideological side by Albert Hourani, *Arabic Thought and the Liberal Age, 1798–1939* (Oxford, 1962) and Hisham Sharabi, *Arab Intellectuals and the West: The Formative Phase, 1875–1914* (Baltimore, 1970).

19. There were some exceptions, particularly in the period of European domination—for example, Taha Hussein and 'Ali 'Abdul Raziq, in their criticism of the prevailing perspective on pre-Islamic civilization and Islamic law, respectively. Taha Hussein, *Concerning Pre-Islamic Literature* (Cairo, 1926) (in Arabic); 'Ali 'Abdul Raziq, *Islam and the Foundation of Government* (Cairo, 1925) (in Arabic). It is noteworthy that Hussein was a graduate of the Sorbonne and 'Abdul Raziq of Oxford; both, however, once over a brief period of youthful defiance, settled into conventional careers, at peace with the status quo. See Hourani, *Arabic Thought,* pp. 327, 216–218.

20. The full social and intellectual consequences of the new linguistic possession did not, however, become apparent until later, with the rise of the critical or radical intellectuals of the 1970s and 1980s. See Chapter 8.

21. For an interesting account of Arab liberalism and its intellectual roots, see 'Ali Umlil, *Arab Reformism and the Nation State* (Beirut, 1985), pp. 153–168 (Arabic). For the younger generation which grew up in the next, postindependence period, this confusing dualism, in which thought seemed to enjoy a separate and autonomous existence, led to a pattern of behavior based on pure action: militancy in the discourse of the period of ideology took the form of violence and terror, not of democracy and humane relations.

Chapter 8

1. A representative sample of such works (all published in Beirut are in Arabic), would include, in the social sciences, Halim Barakat's *Contemporary Arab Society* (Beirut, 1984), the first *comprehensive* sociological study of Arab society, and Ali Zay'our's social psychological study mentioned earlier, *The*

Psychoanalysis of the Arab Self (Beirut, 1977); in political and cultural analysis, 'Abdullah Laroui's *La crise des intellectuelles arabes: Tradionisme ou historicisme* (Paris, 1974); on Muslim culture, the three-volume work by Adonis (Ahmad 'Ali Sa'id), *The Permanent and the Changing: A Study in Imitation and Creativity* (Beirut, 1974–78), Muhammad 'Abid al-Jabiri's "archeological" intellectual history, *The Shaping of the Arab Mind* (Beirut, 1984), Muhammad Arkoun's critical study of Muslim interpretative traditions, *Pour une critique de la raison islamique* (Paris, 1984); in structuralist literary theory, Kamal Abu-Dib, *The Dialectic of Absence and Presence: Structuralist Studies in Poetry* (Beirut, 1979); in Marxist criticism, Sadiq Jalal al-'Azm, *Critique of Religious Thought* (Beirut, 1969); in Marxist dependency theory, Samir Amin's *La nation arabe* (Paris, 1976), and *Classe et nation: dans l'histoire et la crise contemporaine* (Paris, 1979); and Abdelkebir Khatibi's semiological analysis, *La blessure du nom propre* (Paris, 1974), and *Double Critique* (Beirut, 1980), several essays written in French and translated into Arabic. An expanded list would include works (published since 1970) by Saad al-Din Ibrahim and Samih Farsoun (sociology), Hïchem Djaït (history), Sayyid Yasin (social studies), Khalidah Sa'id (literary criticism), Muhammad Jawad Rida (education), and Hanna Batatu (political analysis and social history).

2. *Mawaqif* (October-November, 1969), pp. 3–4.
3. Muhammad 'Abid al-Jabiri, *The Shaping of the Arab Mind* (Beirut, 1984), pp. 11–12 (Arabic). Also see 'Abdul Salim Bin 'Abd al-'Ali, "The Shaping of the Arab Mind," in *al-Ittihad al-Ishtiraki Supplement (Socialist Union)* (Rabat, March 3, 1985), p. 4 (in Arabic).
4. Jabiri, *Formation of the Arab Mind,* p. 6.
5. Ibid.
6. "Rethinking Islam," (Lecture given at Georgetown University, Washington, DC, April 3, 1985).
7. Muhammad Arkoun, *Lectures du Coran* (Paris, 1982), pp. 1–26.
8. Muhammad Arkoun, "Interview," *al-Wihdah* (Paris, December, 1984), p. 130.

9. Ibid., p. 129.

10. *The Crisis of the Arab Intellectuals: Tradition or Historicism,* trans. Diarmid Cammell (Berkeley and Los Angeles, 1976), p. 154.

11. Ibid., p. 154.

12. Ibid., pp. 152–55.

13. Ibid., p. 155.

14. Sadiq al-'Azm, *Critique of Religious Thought* (Beirut, 1969), p. 7 (Arabic).

15. Ibid., p. 8.

16. Ibid.

17. Yasin Hafiz, quoted in ibid., epigraph.

18. "I call *fiqh* all thinking based on 'principles and applications,' 'origins and derivations . . .' for example, the treatment of dialectical materialism by Stalin and his imitators." *al-Wihda* (Paris, October, 1984), p. 28 (Arabic).

19. Ibid., p. 33.

20. Ibid., p. 38.

21. Ibid., p. 29.

22. Ibid.

23. Halim Barakat, *Contemporary Arab Society* (Beirut, 1984), p. 10 (Arabic).

24. Saad al-Din Ibrahim, "Speculation on New Horizons for Arab Sociology," unpublished paper (January, 1985), pp. 8–14 (Arabic).

25. Kamal Abu-Dib, *The Dialectic of Presence and Absence: Structural Studies in Poetry* (Beirut, 1979), p. 7 (Arabic).

26. Ibid., p. 8.

27. See the introduction to the Arabic translation by Muhammad Bennis, *al-Ism al-'Arabi al-Jarih* (*The Wounded Arab Name*) (Beirut, 1980), pp. 5–6.

28. Ibid., pp. 5, 7.

29. Khatibi, *al-Naqd al-Muzdawij* (*Double Critique*), trans. Muhammad Bennis (Beirut, 1980), p. 9.

30. Ibid., p. 157.

31. See, for example, his criticism of Laroui's historicism. Ibid., p. 18.

32. Ibid., pp. 161–162.

33. Ibid., p. 161.
34. Ibid., p. 164.
35. Ibid., p. 158.
36. Ibid., p. 164.
37. Ibid., p. 164.
38. *La blessure du nom propre,* p. 5.
39. Muhammad Bennis, "The Multiplicity of the Single," *al-Karmel (Mt. Carmel)* (1984, n.d.), p. 222 (Arabic).
40. *Double Critique,* p. 31.
41. *al-Muqaddimah* (Beirut, 1970), vol. 1, p. 451.
42. The radical critics (particularly the Maghribi critics) play a role paralleling that of the secular intellectuals of the early part of the Awakening, particularly the Syrian-Lebanese intellectuals. Like the latter, they project a new consciousness at odds with the dominant discourse and oriented toward modernity and change, but with this difference: the Maghribi critics offer a *radical* criticism while their intellectual predecessors only offered a conceptual compromise.
43. The access these Western-trained intellectuals have to German thought, for example, is shaped by the extent and kind of "translation" of the German available in French or English. Thus the knowledge they have of the Frankfurt school, for instance, is determined by the character and orientation of these translations.
44. The best characterization of the West seen in this perspective is still Max Weber's introduction to *The Protestant Ethic and the Spirit of Capitalism* (New York, 1958), pp. 13–31.
45. See Jacques Derrida, *Margins of Philosophy,* trans. Alan Bass (Chicago, 1982), p. 189.
46. Khatibi puts it this way: "Arab knowledge exists only on the outer margins of Western knowledge, and at the same time it cannot think the outside which is its ground." *Double Critique,* p. 164.
47. See Frederic Jameson's critique of Derrida's and Deleuze's detotalizing approach in terms of its incompatibility with the socially fragmented American context. *The Political Unconscious: Narrative as a Symbolic Act* (Ithaca, NY, 1981), p. 54, n. 31.

Chapter 9

1. See S. K. Farsoun, "Class Structure and Social Change in the Arab World," in Hisham Sharabi, ed., *The Next Arab Decade: Alternative Futures* (Boulder, CO, 1988).

2. The bourgeoisie briefly enjoyed tentative ascendancy under European rule and during the early period of independence.

3. Except in the conservative monarchies and the semitribal regimes where it is beginning to enjoy social but not political ascendancy.

4. It is to be recalled that in the second half of the nineteenth century it was the persistence of subsistence farming which obstructed capital accumulation in Turkey and Egypt and forced them to borrow from Europe, thus locking themselves into dependency long before World War I. In Japan, by contrast, where the farmer had been freed from subsistence production in the early seventeenth century and economic surplus was produced very early on, it was possible for the state to invest in industrialization following the Meiji restoration (1866) without having to borrow from Europe.

5. See "Interview with George Qirm," *al-Wihda* (May, 1986), pp. 102–105.

6. In the monarchical and semi-tribal regimes, even though the petty bourgeoisie did not gain political power, its social and cultural dominance, particularly in its fundamentalist form, soon became pervasive, as we shall see.

7. See Keith Griffin and Azizur Rahman Khan, "Poverty and the Third World: Ugly Facts and Fancy Models," in Hamza Alavi and Teodor Shanin, eds., *Introduction to the Sociology of "Developing Societies"* (New York, 1982), p. 247.

8. V. Solodovnikov and V. Bogoslovsky, *Non-Capitalist Development: An Historical Outline* (Moscow, 1975), pp. 236–37.

9. See I. Andreyev, *The Non-Capitalist Way* (Moscow, 1977), pp. 88–96.

10. Solodovnikov and Bogoslovsky, *Non-Capitalist Development*, p. 26.

11. South Yemen's socialist success, like Cuba's, must in part be attributed to its isolation, but also to the unique development of a labor movement in Aden under colonial rule. See Ziyad

Abu-'Amr, *The People's Democratic Republic of Yemen: The Transformation of Society* (Ph.D. diss., Georgetown University, 1986).

12. With the probable exception of Egypt's.

13. 'Abdullah Laroui, *The Concept of the State* (Beirut, 1983), p. 168 (Arabic).

14. This position, for example, was Nasser's in the mid-1960s; at the height of his power he rejected class struggle, maintaining a position of ideological compromise and political pragmatism.

15. Samir Amin, *The Arab Economy Today* (New York, 1982).

16. Ibid., pp. 48, 51.

17. Ibid., p. 56. See also Khalid Tahsin 'Ali, "Disturbing Developments in the Agriculture and Food Production in the Arab World in the 1970s," in Center for Arab Unity Studies, *Studies in Arab Economic Development* (Beirut, 1982), p. 405 (Arabic).

18. Amin, *Arab Economy Today*, p. 56.

19. Ibid., p. 60.

20. Ibid., p. 66.

21. Ibid., p. 69. The amount of "qualified" labor, defined in terms of technical or advanced education, as compared to unskilled labor, defined in terms of illiterate or primary level of education, was 4.8 and 87 percent, respectively, of the total Arab labor force.

22. Arab enterprise, whether in the private or the public sector, became fully dependent on the multinational corporations. Ibid., p. 73.

23. Ibid., pp. 76–78.

24. Ibid., p. 78.

25. In instances of mass or national upheaval rallying around a party or movement (the Wafd under Saad, the Nasserist movement), it was the charisma of the leader or a national crisis which brought this about, not ideological commitment or party mobilization and organization.

26. For an example of such a reading, see Emmanuel Sivan, *Radical Islam, Medieval Theology, and Modern Politics* (New Haven, 1985).

27. He was executed in 1964 in Cairo on a conspiracy charge.

28. Sayyid Qutb, *Landmarks on the Way* (Cairo, 1972), p. 105 (Arabic).

29. Qutb's view of existing (neopatriarchal) society as a form of *jahiliyyah* is significant for fundamentalism's justification of revolt and the use of violence. "All that surrounds us is *jahiliyyah*, people's visions, beliefs, their habits and customs, their source of knowledge, art, literature, rules and laws, Islamic sources, Islamic philosophy and Islamic thought—all of it is the product of *jahiliyyah*," quoted in Yvonne Y. Haddad, "Sayyid Qutb: Ideologue of Islamic Revival," in John L. Esposito, ed., *Voices of Resurgent Islam* (New York, 1983), p. 85.

30. An extreme expression of born-again Muslims may be seen in the attitude and (near-hysterical) discourse of female coverts identifying with a phallocentric ideology.

31. Qutb, *Landmarks*, p. 105.

32. Quoted in Haddad, "Sayyid Qutb," p. 83.

33. Qutb, *Landmarks*, p. 96.

34. Here the knowledge/power model finds its clearest expression in fundamentalism.

35. 'Abdul Muhsin al-Nimr, *Islam and the West* (Cairo, 1983), p. 15 (Arabic).

36. See *Declaration and Program of the Syrian Islamic Revolution* (Damascus, 1980), p. 2 (Arabic).

37. Hassan al-Banna, *The Three Letters* (Cairo, 1977), p. 16 (Arabic).

38. Qutb, *Landmarks*, p. 14.

39. *Declaration and Program*, p. 62.

40. Ibid.

41. al-Banna, *The Three Letters*, p. 81.

42. Ibid., p. 84.

43. Ibid., pp. 85–99.

44. Ibid., p. 104.

45. Ibid., p. 108.

46. Ibid., pp. 109–110.

47. Ibid., pp. 110–114.

48. Ibid., pp. 114–116.

Chapter 10

1. *The Middle East and Sweden's Security,* National Defense Research Institute (Stockholm, 1985). For selections from the report, see *Journal of Palestine Studies* (Summer, 1985), pp. 106–16.
2. *The Arab Nation,* trans. Michael Pallis (London, 1978), p. 112.
3. Ibid., p. 114.
4. Unpublished Proceedings of the "Symposium on the Social Sciences in the Arab World," Tunis, January 25–28, 1985, pp. 2–3.
5. Georg Lukacs, *Studies in European Realism* (New York, 1964), p. 10.

Bibliography

'Abdel-Nasser, Jamal. *A Collection of Speeches, Declarations, and Documents*. Cairo: Dar al-Tali'a, 1964 (Arabic).

'Abdel-Malek, Anouar. *Egypt: Military Society: the Army Regime, the Left, and Social Change under Nasser*. Translated by Charles Lam Markmann. New York: Random House, 1968.

'Abdullah, 'Abdul-Khaleq. "Political Dependency: The Case of the United Arab Emirates." Ph.D. dissertation, Georgetown University, 1984.

Abu-'Amr, Ziad. "The Peoples' Democratic Republic of Yemen: The Transformation of Society." Ph.D. dissertation, Georgetown University, 1985.

Abu-Dib, Kamal. *The Dialectic of Absence and Presence: Structuralist Studies in Poetry*. Beirut: Dar al-'Ilm lil-Malayin, 1979 (Arabic).

Adonis. *The Permanent and the Changing: A Study in Imitation and Creativity*. 3 vols. Beirut: Dar al-'Awdah (1974–1978 Arabic).

Alavi, Hamza, and Teodor Shanin, eds. *Introduction to the Sociology of "Developing Societies."* New York: Monthly Review Press, 1982.

Althusser, Louis. *Pour Marx*. Paris: F. Maspero, 1965. Translated by Ben Brewster. *For Marx*. London: Penguin, 1969.

Amin, Samir, *La nation arabe*. Paris: Editions des Minuit, 1976. Translated by Michael Pollis. *The Arab Nation*. London: Zed Press, 1978.

————. *Classes et nation: dans l'histoire et la crise contemporaine.* Paris: Editions des Minuit, 1979. Translated by Susan Kaplow. *Class and Nation, Historically and in the Current Crisis.* New York: Monthly Review Press, 1980.

————. "The Middle East Crisis in Its World Framework." *al-Mustaqbal al-'Arabi* (*Arab Future*), (August 1983), pp. 22–32 (Arabic).

Anderson, Perry. *Considerations on Western Marxism.* London: New Left Books, 1976.

————. *In the Tracks of Historical Materialism.* Chicago: University of Chicago Press, 1984.

————. *Lineages of the Absolute State.* London: New Left Books, 1974.

Antonius, Soraya. *The Lord.* London: Hamish Hamilton, 1985.

al-'Aqqad, 'Abbas Mahmud. *Intellectual Doctrines of the Twentieth Century.* Cairo: Maktabat Gharib, 1968 (Arabic).

Arkoun, Mohammad. *Lèctures du Coran.* Paris: Maisonneuve et Larose, 1982.

————. *Pour une critique de la raison islamique.* Paris: Maisonneuve et Larose, 1984.

————. "Rethinking Islam." Lecture at Georgetown University, October 30, 1985.

Arnove, Robert F. *Philanthropy and Cultural Imperialism: The Foundations at Home and Abroad.* Bloomington: Indiana University Press, 1982.

al-'Azm Sadiq Jalal. *Critique of Religious Thought.* Beirut: Dar al-Tal: 'ah, 1969 (Arabic).

al-Banna, Hassan. *The Three Letters.* Cairo: Dar al-Tiba'ah wal-Nashr al-Islamiyyah, 1977 (Arabic).

Barakat, Halim. *Contemporary Arab Society: A Social Exploratory Study.* Beirut: Center for Arab Unity Studies, 1984 (Arabic).

Barthes, Roland. *Critical Essays.* Translated by Richard Howard. Evanston, IL: Northwestern University Press, 1972.

————. *Elements of Semiology.* Translated by Annette Lavers and Colin Smith. New York: Hill and Wang, 1968.

————. *The Pleasure of the Text.* Translated by Richard Miller. New York: Hill and Wang, 1975.

Batatu, Hanna. *The Old Social Classes and the Revolutionary*

Movements of Iraq: A Study of Iraq's Old Landed and Commercial Classes and of Its Communists, Ba'thists, and Free Officers. Princeton: Princeton University Press, 1978.

Berman, Marshall. *All That Is Solid Melts into Air: The Experience of Modernity.* New York: Simon and Schuster, 1982.

Berque, Jacques. *Les Arabes.* Paris: Editions Sindbad, 1979.

———. *The Arabs: Their History and Future.* Translated by Jean Stewart. London: Faber and Faber, 1964.

Bloch, Marc L. B. *Feudal Society.* 2 vols. Translated by L. A. Manyon. Chicago: University of Chicago Press, 1961.

Blomström, Magnus, and Hettne Björn. *Development Theory in Transition: The Dependency Debate and Beyond: Third World Responses.* London: Zed Press, 1984.

Braudel, Fernand. *Capitalism and Material Life, 1400–1800.* Translated by Miriam Kochan. New York: Harper and Row, 1973.

Callinicos, Alex. *Marxism and Philosophy.* New York: Oxford University Press, 1983.

Carnoy, Martin. *Education as Cultural Imperialism.* New York: D. McKay, 1974.

Castoriadis, Cornelius. *The Imaginary Institution of Society.* Translated by Kathleen Blamey. Oxford: Polity, 1987.

Cohen, Gerald Allen. *Karl Marx's Theory of History: A Defense.* Princeton: Princeton University Press, 1978.

Darwazah, H. *Local Communism and the National Arab Battle.* Beirut, 1961 (Arabic).

Deleuze, Gilles, and Felix Guattari. *Anti-Oedipus: Capitalism and Schizophrenia.* Translated by Robert Hurley, Mark Seem, and Helen R. Lane. New York: Viking Press, 1977.

Derrida, Jacques. *Of Grammatology.* Translated by Gayatri Spivak. Baltimore: Johns Hopkins University Press, 1976.

———. *Positions.* Translated by Alan Bass. Chicago: University of Chicago Press, 1981.

———. *Writing and Difference.* Translated by Alan Bass. Chicago: Chicago University Press, 1978.

———. *Margins of Philosophy.* Translated by Alan Bass. Chicago: University of Chicago Press, 1982.

Djaït, Hichem. *Europe and Islam.* Translated by Peter Heinegg. Berkeley: University of California Press, 1985.

Dodge, Bayard. *The American University of Beirut*. Beirut: Khayyat's, 1958.

Donohue, John J., and John L. Esposito, eds. *Islam in Transition*. New York: Oxford University Press, 1982.

Dowling, William C. *Jameson, Althusser, Marx: An Introduction to the Political Unconscious*. Ithaca, NY: Cornell University Press, 1984.

Erikson, Erik H. *Young Man Luther: A Study in Psychoanalysis and History*. New York: Norton, 1958.

Esposito, John L., ed. *Voices of Resurgent Islam*. New York: Oxford University Press, 1983.

Fanon, Frantz. *Black Skin, White Masks*. Translated by Charles Lam Markmann. New York: Grove Press, 1967.

———. *A Dying Colonialism*. Translated by Haakon Chevalier. New York: Grove Press, 1965.

Farah, Elyas. *The Evolution of Marxist Thought*. Beirut: Dar al-Tali'ah, 1968 (Arabic).

Farsoun, Samih K., and Walter F. Carroll. "State Capitalism and Counterrevolution in the Middle East: A Thesis," in Barbara Kaplan, ed. *Social Change in the Capitalist World Economy*. Beverly Hills, CA: Sage Publications, 1978.

Fernea, Elizabeth Warnok, and Basima Qattan Bezirgan, eds. *Middle Eastern Muslim Women Speak*. Austin: University of Texas Press, 1977.

Foucault, Michel. *The Archeology of Knowledge*. Translated by A. M. Sheridan Smith. New York: Harper and Row, 1972.

———. *The Order of Things: An Archaeology of the Human Sciences*. New York: Pantheon, 1970.

Freire, Paulo. *Pedagogy of the Oppressed*. Translated by Myra Bergman Ramos. New York: Herder and Herder, 1970.

Haddad, Nicola. "Socialism" (1920), in *Roots of Socialism*. Beirut: Dar al-Tali'ah, 1964 (Arabic).

al-Hakim, Tawfiq. *Letters and Documents*. Cairo: Dar al-Ma'arif, 1975 (Arabic).

———. *The Return of Consciousness*. Translated by R. Baley Winder. New York: New York University Press, 1985.

Hoffman, John. *The Gramscian Challenge: Coercion and Consent in Marxist Political Theory*. Oxford: Blackwell, 1984.

Hsu, Francis L. K. *Under the Ancestor's Shadow: Chinese Cul-*

ture and Personality. New York: Columbia University Press, 1948.

Hussein, Taha. *Memoirs*. Beirut: Dar al-Adab, 1967 (Arabic).

———. *On Pre-Islamic Literature*. Cairo: Dar al-Ma'arif, 1964 (Arabic).

Ibrahim, Ibrahim, ed. *Arab Resources: The Transformation of a Society*. Washington, DC: Georgetown University, Center for Contemporary Arab Studies, 1983.

Saad al-Din Ibrahim. *The New Arab Order: A Study of the Social Impact of Oil Wealth*. London: Croom Helm, 1982.

al-Jabarti, 'Abd al-Rahman. *History of Egypt*. Vol. 1. Cairo: Lajnat al-Bayan al-'Arabi, 1958 (Arabic).

al-Jabiri, Muhammad 'Abid. *The Shaping of the Arab Mind*. Beirut: Dar al-Tali'ah, 1984 (Arabic).

———. *Contemporary Arab Public Address*. Beirut: Dar al-Tali'ah, 1982 (Arabic).

Jameson, Frederic. *The Political Unconscious: Narrative as a Socially Symbolic Act*. Ithaca, NY: Cornell University Press, 1981.

———. *The Prison-House of Language*. Princeton: Princeton University Press, 1972.

———. "Marxism and Historicism." *New Literary History* (Autumn, 1979), pp. 41–73.

Joseph, Roger. "Toward a Semiotics of Middle Eastern Culture." *International Journal of Middle East Studies* (November 1980), pp. 319–29.

al-Khalidi, Mustafa, and 'Umar Farroukh. *The Missionary Movements and Colonialism*. Beirut: al-Maktabah al-'ilmiyyah, 1953 (Arabic).

Ibn Khaldun. *al-Maqaddimah*. 2 vols. Beirut: Dar al-Hayat, 1970. Translated by Franz Rosenthal. *An Introduction to History*. 2nd ed. Princeton: Princeton University Press, 1967.

Khatibi, Abdekebir. *La blessure du nom propre*. Paris: Denoël, 1974. Translated into Arabic by Muhammad Bennis.

———. *Double Critique*. Translated into Arabic by Muhammad Bennis. Beirut: Dar al-'Awdah, 1980.

Kuhn, Thomas S. *The Structure of Scientific Revolutions*. Chicago: University of Chicago Press, 1962.

Lacan, Jacques. *Ecrits: A Selection*. Translated by Alan Sheridan. New York: Norton, 1977.

———. *The Four Fundamental Concepts of Psycho-analysis*. Edited by Jacques-Alain Miller. Translated by Alan Sheridan. New York: Norton, 1977.

Lambton, Ann K. S. *State and Government in Medieval Islam: An Introduction to the Study of Islamic Political Theory: the Jurists*. New York: Oxford University Press, 1981.

Laroui, 'Abdullah. *The Concept of the State*. Beirut: Dar al-Haqiqah, 1973 (Arabic).

———. *The Concept of Ideology*. Beirut: Dar al-Haqiqah, 1983 (Arabic).

———. *The Concept of Freedom*. Beirut: Dar al-Haqiqah, 1983 (Arabic).

———. *La crise des intellectuelles arabes: Traditionalisime on historicisme*. Paris: Librarie François Maspero, 1974.

———. *The Crisis of the Arab Intellectuals: Tradition or Historicism*. Translated by Diarmid Cammell. Berkeley and Los Angeles: University of California Press, 1976.

Lichtman, Richard. *The Production of Desire: The Integration of Psychoanalysis and Marxist Theory*. New York: Free Press, 1982.

Lukacs, Georg. *The Destruction of Reason*. Translated by Peter Palmer. Atlantic Heights, NJ: Humanities Press, 1981.

de Man, Paul. *Blindness and Insight: Essays in the Rhetoric of Contemporary Criticism*. Minneapolis: University of Minnesota Press, 1983.

Mandel, Ernest. *Marxist Economic Theory*. Translated by Brian Pearce. New York: Monthly Review Press, 1968.

al-Manfaluti, Mustafah Lutfi, *Virtue*. Beirut: Dar al-Thaqafah, 1968 (Arabic).

Marlowe, John. *Perfidious Albion: The Origins of Anglo-French Rivalry in the Levant*. London: Elek, 1971.

Marx, Karl. *Capital*. Vol. 1. New York: The Modern Library, 1906.

———. *Grundrisse*. Translated by Martin Nicolaus. London: Penguin, 1970.

———. *Karl Marx: On Society and Social Change*. Neil J. Smelser, ed. Chicago: University of Chicago Press, 1973.

————. *The German Ideology*. New York: International Publishers, 1967.

Massialas, Byron G., and Samir Ahmed Jarrar. *Education in the Arab World*. New York: Praeger, 1983.

al-Mazini, Ibrahim. *Barren Harvest*. Cairo: al-Dar al-Qawmiyyah, 1948 (Arabic).

Melotti, Umberto. *Marx and the Third World*. Translated by Pat Ransford. Edited by Malcolm Caldwell. London: Macmillan, 1977.

Memmi, Albert. *The Colonizer and the Colonized*. Translated by Howard Greenfeld. New York: Orion Press, 1965.

Merleau-Ponty, Maurice. *Humanism and Terror: An Essay on the Communist Problem*. Translated by John O'Neill. Boston: Beacon Press, 1969.

Monroe, Elizabeth. *Britain's Moment in the Middle East, 1914–1917*. Baltimore: Johns Hopkins University Press, 1981.

Mowlana, Hamid. *Global Information and World Communication: New Frontiers in International Relations*. New York: Longman, 1986.

Murad, Hussein, Mahmoud Amin al-ʿAlim, Mohammed Dirkamb, and Samir Saʿd. *Studies of Islam*. Jerusalem: Salah al-Din, 1980 (Arabic).

Murqus, Elyas. *Marxism in Our Time*. Beirut: Dar al-Taliʿah, 1969 (Arabic).

Musa, Salamah. "Socialism" (1913), in *Roots of Socialism*. Beirut: Dar al-Taliʿah, 1964 (Arabic).

Owen, Roger. *The Middle East in the World Economy, 1800–1914*. London: Methuen, 1981.

————, and Bob Sutcliffe, eds. *Studies in the Theory of Imperialism*. London: Longman, 1972.

Penrose, Stephen B. L. *That They May Have Life: The Story of the American University of Beirut, 1866–1941*. New York: The Trustees of the American University of Beirut, 1941.

Piaget, Jean. *The Essential Piaget*. Edited by Howard E. Guber and J. Jacques Vonèche. New York: Basic Books, 1977.

Preiswerk, Roy, and Dominique Perrot. *Ethnocentrism and History: Africa, Asia and Indian America in Western Textbooks*. New York: NOK Publishers International, 1978.

Qutb, Sayyid. *Landmarks on the Road*. Cairo: Dar al-Shuruq, 1972 (Arabic). Translated by S. Badrul Hasan. *Milestones*. Karachi: International Islamic Publishers, 1981.

Reich, Wilhelm. *The Sexual Revolution: Toward a Self-Regulating Character Structure*. Translated by Theodore P. Wolfe. New York: Simon and Schuster, 1974.

Rida, Muhammad J. *Philosophy of Education*. Kuwait: Kuwait University Press, 1972 (Arabic).

Rudich, Norman, ed. *Weapons of Criticism: Marxism in America and the Literary Tradition*. Palo Alto, CA: Ramparts Press, 1976.

Ryan, Michael. *Marxism and Deconstruction: A Critical Articulation*. Baltimore: Johns Hopkins University Press, 1982.

Sa'id, Rif'at. *Leftist Media in Egypt, 1925–1948*. 2nd ed. Cairo: Dar al-Thaqafah al-Jadidah, 1977 (Arabic).

Samater, Ibrahim. "From 'Growth' to 'Basic Needs': The Evolution of Development Theory." *Monthly Review* (October, 1984), pp. 1–13.

de Saint Pierre, Bernardin. *Paul et Virginie*. Paris: A. Quantin, 1878.

Sa'id, Khalidah. *Dynamics of Creativity: Studies in Modern Arabic Literature*. Beirut: Dar al-'Awdah, 1979 (Arabic).

Schiller, Herbert I. *The Mind Managers*. Boston: Beacon Press, 1973.

al-Sharqawi, Mahmud. *Salamah Musa: the Thinker and the Man*. Beirut: Dar Al-'ilm lil-Malayin, 1965 (Arabic).

Smith, Anthony. *The Geopolitics of Information: How Western Culture Dominates the World*. New York: Oxford University Press, 1980.

Smith, Thomas C. *The Agrarian Origins of Modern Japan*. Stanford: Stanford University Press, 1959.

Solodovnikov, V., and V. Bogoslovsky. *Non-Capitalist Development: An Historical Outline*. Translated by A. Bratov. Moscow: Progress Publishers, 1975.

Slovo, Joe. "A Critical Appraisal of the Non-Capitalist Path and the National Democratic State in Africa." *Marxism Today* (June 1974), pp. 175–88.

Swartz, Merlin, *Studies on Islam*. New York: Oxford University Press, 1981.

Sweet, Louise E., ed. *The Central Middle East: A Handbook of*

Anthropology and Published Research on the Nile Valley, the Arab Levant, Southern Mesopotamia, the Arabian Peninsula, and Israel. New Haven, CT: Hraf Press, 1971.

Taymur, Mahmoud. *International Literature.* Cairo: Maktabat al-Adab, 1959 (Arabic).

Tazzini, Tayyib. *From Legacy to Revolution.* Beirut: Dar Ibn-Khaldoun, 1978 (Arabic).

Thomas, Clive Y. "The Non-Capitalist Path as Theory and Practice of Decolonization and Socialist Transformation." *Latin American Perspectives* (Spring, 1978), pp. 10–28.

Trumbach, Randolph. *The Rise of the Egalitarian Family: Aristocratic Kinship and Domestic Relations in Eighteenth-Century England.* New York: Academic Press, 1978.

Tsurumi, Kazuko. *Social Change and the Individual: Japan Before and After Defeat in World War II.* Princeton: Princeton University Press, 1970.

Tunis University, Center for Economic and Social Research. *The Arabs Before Their Fate.* Tunis: Tunis University, 1980 (Arabic).

Umlil, 'Ali. *Arab Reformism and the Nation State.* Beirut, 1985 (Arabic).

Watt, W. Montgomery. *Muhammad at Medina.* Oxford: Clarendon Press, 1956.

Wexler, Philip. *Critical Social Psychology.* London: Routledge and Kegan Paul, 1983.

Wickwar, William Hardy. *The Modernization of Administration in the Near East.* Beirut: Khayyat's, 1963.

Yasin, Sayyid. *The Arab Personality.* Beirut: Dar al-Tanwir, 1981 (Arabic).

Zay'our, Ali. *The Psychoanalysis of the Arab Self.* Beirut: Dar al-Tali'ah, 1977 (Arabic).

Zhuze, Pantele. *From the History of Intellectual Movements in Islam.* 3rd ed. Jerusalem: Matba'at Beit al-Quds, 1928 (Arabic).

Zureik, Elia. *The Palestinians in Israel: A Study in Internal Colonialism.* London: Routledge and Kegan Paul, 1979.

Zwemer, Samuel M. *Childhood in the Moslem World.* New York: Fleming H. Revell, 1915.

Zygmunt G. Baranski, and John R. Short, eds. *Developing Contemporary Marxism.* New York: St. Martin's Press, 1985.

Index

'Abdul Raziq, 'Ali, 168n19
Adonis, 104–5
'Ailah (extended family), 31–32
Algeria, 69, 70, 72, 128, 164n7
American educational foundations,
  82–83
Amin, Samir, 49, 51, 52, 54, 133–35,
  149, 163n3
Anarchism, 124
Antonius, Soraya, 77
Appearance vs. reality, under
  etatism, 66
al-'Aqqad, 'Abbas, 102
Arab Awakening *(nahda)*
  European imperialism and,
    67–70
  ideology vs. epistemology in, 101
  Islamic fundamentalism and, 136
  Islamic reformism and, 74
  language of, 167n17
  missionary education and, 79
  modernity and, 6, 98–99
  neopatriarchal society and, 4, 6–9
  political ideology and, 58
  and secularism vs. Islam, 10–11,
    80
  terms of modernity and, 91–92
Arab Economy Today, The (Amin),
  133–35
Arabic. *See also* Classical Arabic;
  Language

modern, 117–18
"newspaper," 97–98, 118
Arab Organization for Human
  Rights, 154
Arab patriarchy
  characteristics of, 16–17
  stages and types of, 26–27
  women's place in, 32–34
Arab society. *See also* Neopatriarchal society
  American foundations in, 82–83
  capitalism in, 5–6
  colonized vs. dependent countries
    in, 61–63
  demographic features of, 16
  as European creation, 67–70
  fundamentalist solution for, 11,
    140–43
  fundamentalist view of, 143–47
  geographic features of, 16
  hindrance to socio-political
    change in, 74
  political life in, under petty
    bourgeoisie, 9
  solution to problems in, 11, 99,
    140–43, 150
  survival of, 151–52
  underlying structures in, 23–24
Arab world. *See* Arab society
Arkoun, Muhammad, 117
'Ashirah (subtribe), 31

187